Lillian Too's

smart feng shui for the home

Lillian Too's
smart feng shui for the home

188 brilliant ways to work
with what you've got

Lillian Too

ELEMENT

Element
An Imprint of HarperCollinsPublishers
77–85 Fulham Palace Road
Hammersmith, London W6 8JB

First published in Great Britain in 2001 by
Element Books Limited

10 9 8 7 6 5 4 3 2 1

Publishing Director: Belinda Budge
Project Manager: Liz Dean
Designer: Ann Burnham
Senior Production Controller: Mell Vandevelde
Text illustrations by Joan Corlass

A catalogue record for this book
is available from the British Library

ISBN 0 0071 1750 7

Printed and bound in Great Britain by Scotprint

dedication

For my daughter Jennifer, and my nephew Han Jin –
two beautiful people who give me much joy.

acknowledgements

I want to thank all the wonderful people behind this very cleverly produced book – to Liz Dean, who has become a dear friend – she has literally worked overtime on this book; to the illustrator she found for us, and to the wonderful team at Thorsons – Nicky Vimpany, Jo Ridgeway, Melanie Vandevelde and Catherine Forbes. They have done a brilliant job despite working under impossible deadlines. Thank you my dears for bending backwards to ensure accuracy and authenticity. This makes such difference.

Mostly I want to thank Belinda Budge, my new Publishing Director, who brought her experience and her skill towards the conception and design of this book, so that the end result is a meaty book that is practical, original, simple, beautifully designed, and easy on the pocket book as well. I am really proud and honored to be working with so many excellent professional people.

Lillian Too's author website is at www.lillian-too.com
Her feng shui magazine website is at www.wofs.com
The feng shui mall is at www.fsmegamall.com
The feng shui greeting cards site is at www.fsgreetings.com
note: all letters and emails may be addressed to ltoo@wofs.com

contents

introduction

Feng shui does not have to be difficult for it to work. My approach to feng shui has always been based on this premise, so I always write with this in mind. I judge the success of my books not on how many copies they sell, but on how successful I have been in making feng shui easy to understand.

The key to good feng shui is of course to practice it correctly, so simplifying it means that I ensure that the essence of its concepts and fundamental theories is never sacrificed. Happily, when one's knowledge of a subject has been tried and tested continuously, one emerges with a sharper and more accurate view of the subject; hence the task of simplification becomes easier.

In this book I have tried to create a window for you into the world of chi energy (what we Chinese call the dragon's cosmic breath,) and share with you a fresh way of looking at the shapes and colors that surround you, and at the decorative objects and the art you hang on your walls. Hopefully, too, I can persuade you to assess the arrangement of your furniture with new feng shui eyes, and alert you to the hidden dangers in your home created by poisonous and killing energy in your space.

As you read about all the simple things you can do immediately to improve your feng shui, do not think that the Tips contained here are any less potent than those you read about in my more advanced books on feng shui. The practice of feng shui operates on many different levels. It has tremendous depth, and there are multiple layers of interpretation and subtle nuances of meaning. However, in my quest for deeper knowledge, I have discovered that the most spectacular success

has been when I never forget to observe the simple guidelines of feng shui. Even when I practice the more complicated formulas, I find it is when I systematically break them down into bite-sized steps that I get things done correctly. And then feng shui seems to work for me in a most spectacular fashion.

This is what I am attempting to share with you in this book.

This book presents all the essential information you will need to feng shui your environment correctly and successfully. I have included simplified applications of formulas, arranged into manageable Tips, so you can use all of my recommendations with peace of mind. Even those of you living in the Southern hemisphere can practice the Tips as they stand – there is no need to change any of the directions given.

But do take note of some simple preliminaries. Read the first chapter carefully. Learn how to choose and use a good compass. Learn to take the directions of your house accurately. Learn how to demarcate the compass sectors of your home in the correct way. Familiarize yourself with the basic attributes and associations of the eight directions of the compass. Work through any mental blocks you may have against understanding numbers, and learn to love the Lo Shu Square. Develop a mental affinity with the eight basic trigrams so you know immediately what each stands for in terms of feng shui significance. And then you will be ready to begin.

Working with what you've got

This book highlights the most important practices and formulas that you can put to work immediately. I will show you how to make feng shui changes that are completely within your control, and which will not break your budget. This is not a book for the wealthy who can afford to completely demolish their homes and build anew from the ground up. This is a book for the majority of us who do have some physical and financial constraints, so we have to work with what we've got. It is especially suitable for couples who are beginning life together in a new home. I believe that things usually start to go bad in these relationships when the feng shui of their new home is out of sync.

Usually, they start out very much in love with each other. Things should not go wrong between them unless the chi energy that surrounds them causes arguments, misunderstandings, fights and, even worse, infidelity and a break-up of the relationship. So it is worthwhile getting the living space arranged in a way that is not only conducive to success, but also brings about continued happiness.

This book is also for young professionals just starting out on new careers and getting a taste of independence. For them it is a good idea to let feng shui help rather than hinder, especially when it is so easy to practice. If you live in an apartment and have little control over the larger environment around your building, you can try to do what you can to ensure that the small space represented by your home stays balanced, harmonious, and a haven from the vagaries of the outside environment. This way you make the best of what you've got.

Many of the Tips contained in these pages apply to the interior of your home, and to spaces that are within your control. You will, of course, come across feng shui afflictions where the cure suggested simply cannot be implemented in your situation. However, there is no need to panic when this happens. I want to assure you that no one in this world has perfect feng shui. Everyone has something or other wrong with their feng shui, so it is necessary to take a "big picture" approach. To do this, you need to consider two special feng shui concepts. These are the space dimension and time dimension.

The nature of chi is that it is continuously in a state of change. And so the chi of any living space is subject to small, but imperceptibly shifting, forces. The key to feng shui success is therefore to arrange your space as best you can, given the physical constraints of your home and the budgetary constraints of your pocket, and then to take careful note of the time taboos – the change of chi patterns that affect the energy of your home from year to year.

In Chapter 8 I have simplified the application of time dimensional feng shui forces that change each year (see Tips 182–188.) Overcoming the afflictions of time on your feng shui is not difficult to do. You simply have to observe certain annual taboos, and place specific antidotes to the afflicted sectors of your home, paying particular attention to those areas that feature strongly in feng shui manifestations of good and bad luck.

An attitude for success

At all times you should have a very relaxed attitude and enjoy the practice of feng shui. Do not conjure unhealthy and ridiculous expectations in your mind. Feng shui cannot create instant miracles. It cannot make you win the lottery – it won't bring immediate wealth or a new love relationship overnight. But yes, good feng shui works pretty fast in that it often takes only nine days for you to notice a difference in the chi within your home.

Also, take note that feng shui accounts for only one-third of your luck – our "earth luck." The other components of one's destiny is the "heaven luck" that you are born with – one's fate, karma, or fortune as written in the stars (that part of our luck over which we have little control,) and what I term our own intrinsic "mankind luck" – the luck that we create as a result of actions and attitudes. This, like feng shui luck, is the type of luck over which we have control. So, when you practice feng shui with a healthy, positive attitude, the possibility of fast, direct benefits increases tremendously.

I have to say that I have always practiced feng shui with the kind of motivation which I believe enhances its power even more – in that for me, feng shui is merely a means to an end. I use feng shui to improve the quality of my relationships, to bring happiness to members of my immediate and extended family, and to make my life more meaningful and fulfilled by being able to make a positive difference to the everyday lives of others.

So for me personally, feng shui has brought a fulfillment way beyond my wildest dreams.

Today I am doing what I truly love – which is writing good, successful books on subjects with which I feel an affinity, and which I know have the potential to bring great measures of delight and happiness to others. Feng shui is one of my favorite subjects simply because it is both fascinating and potent. What has been quite amazing to me is its stunning depth. Feng shui can be approached from so many angles and in such a variety of ways. I am continually learning and, the more I learn, the more I realize how little I know in the vast world of knowledge that feng shui represents.

Like an onion, feng shui represents a wonderful sphere of knowledge; its philosophy, rituals, and symbols represent layer upon layer of marvellous new horizons. The scope of the practice is truly remarkable. So with this book I invite you to take your first tentative steps into the world of feng shui or, if you are already a practitioner, to benefit equally from the Tips contained within.

I want you to taste the potency of feng shui and enjoy healthy, friendly, and auspicious chi in your space before going deeper. I hope that this book brings you many moments of enjoyment as you improve the chi of your space. More importantly, I ask that the Tips in this book will answer the prayers of those most in need of feng shui help.

You can write to me at my email address, ltoo@wofs.com. I can't answer all my letters, but I do read them. Please ensure your letter is not more than fifty words, and I will try to reply.

Lillian Too, Kuala Lumpur October 2000

1

smart

feng shui

basics

1 a feng shui view of the living space

As the world becomes increasingly familiarized with feng shui, this ancient Chinese practice brings ever-growing benefits to those who apply it in their homes.

Feng shui, which literally means wind and water, promises a way of arranging space so that it brings residents good fortune while simultaneously reducing misfortune. Feng shui has gained popularity because many people are discovering that it works, and that it does not have to be difficult to bring fast results. It is easy to use at different levels, and many people are now convinced that at least some working knowledge of feng shui is necessary when setting up home, buying a new home or simply assessing one's existing living space. It is becoming so sought after that people are finding themselves wishing that they knew exactly how to get started without having to plough through reams of books and, more importantly, without getting confused by the proliferation of feng shui literature now available.

This book on easy and practical feng shui deals with feng shui that is within the control of the average person. Solutions to feng shui afflictions usually take account of practical considerations – after all, we must work with what we've got. So space limitations, general immovability of doors, the presence of overhead beams, of missing corners and so forth, which often represent afflictions one cannot do much about, have a lower priority here than those aspects of the practice that can be more easily applied, thereby enhancing your feng shui overall.

Start by understanding that there are four different aspects to the practice of feng shui: exterior feng shui, interior feng shui, the importance of orientations, and time dimension feng shui, which are dealt with separately in the next four Tips.

With your floor plan and the orientations of important rooms, you can improve your feng shui.

- Note some impressions – look at the size, shape, and flow of chi, or energy, within the home.
- Take the orientation of the main door and see if anything is hurting it.
- Get yourself oriented correctly. Use a compass to mark out the different sectors.
- Superimpose the directions onto a floor plan of your home, and note the compass sector of important rooms.

Feng shui at home begins with a floor plan.

2   the first aspect: exterior feng shui

This is the feng shui of the outside environment that surrounds an office building or your home. Different factors are considered that can affect whether the site is considered auspicious.

Exterior feng shui involves assessing a landscape in order to study the effects of mountains, hills, rivers waterways, roads, shapes, and the configuration of contours.

The external view gives you a bigger picture of feng shui, but your surroundings are usually way outside the average person's control. Even when you know how to detect good and bad landscape feng shui, you are seldom in a position to do much about it. In modern-day living, especially in towns and cities, the practice of landscape feng shui often presents insurmountable physical and budgetary constraints.

Old traditions

The Chinese believe that every site is surrounded by four protective animal spirits: the black tortoise, the phoenix, the green dragon, and the white tiger. When a site is being assessed, the four animal names may be applied to the four points of

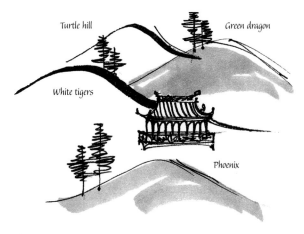

The four celestial creatures of exterior feng shui are the black turtle behind a dwelling, the greek dragon on the left, the white tiger to its right, and the red phoenix in front. Their symbolic presence brings good fortune.

the compass – so that north is the black tortoise, south is the phoenix, east is the green dragon, and west is the white tiger. The superior dragon hill needs to be higher and more rugged than the tiger hill. The southern, phoenix aspect should be open.

The white tiger is the embodiment of yin energy. It complements the yang of the green dragon.

3 the second aspect: interior feng shui

This is taking a detailed feng shui perspective of an interior setting, looking at the chi energy flow inside houses, apartments, and office buildings.

This deals with the layout of rooms, the flow of traffic, the arrangement of furniture, the selection of colors, shapes, dimensions, and decorative materials to ensure that auspicious chi gets created within homes, and inside the rooms of offices and apartments. Interior feng shui is usually well within the control of most people. From a practical perspective, this is the branch of feng shui practice that offers the most scope for individual solutions and creativity. Taking a feng shui view of the living space therefore is primarily about interior feng shui.

In interior feng shui, the front door should open inwards. An auspicious painting in the hall, such as this fish, symbolizes wealth coming into the mouth of the home.

Rooms in the house

Interior feng shui involves looking at the position and orientation of the front door, how the chi energy flows in, and how it enters all the rooms in the house. Any obstructions, such as pillars, beams, or badly placed staircases, are neutralized with feng shui cures such as windchimes, crystals, and plants. It is learning to train your eye so that you can easily spot problems in each area or room of your home, knowing how to position your bed auspiciously, and hang mirrors to advantage.

Check out the view from your front door. A curved path and healthy plants bring in good chi energy, while a straight path or telegraph poles will create negative chi for your home.

4 the third aspect: the importance of orientations

In Chinese feng shui, all the compass orientations of a house, apartment, or office play the largest and most crucial role in correct feng shui practice.

It is vital to establish orientations correctly before powerfully potent feng shui formulas can be correctly activated to bring fast results. This requires the use of a reliable compass and some basic reference points with which to demarcate your living and work areas. This can collectively be called the space dimension of interior feng shui, and to a very large extent this too is within the control of most people. So when you want to feng shui any living space, one of the first things you absolutely must take account of is the relative orientation of rooms, of doors, and furniture placement.

Taking a feng shui view of any space should always include input on orientations.

Using a compass

As is mentioned later in the book, you need to use a good Western compass to find out the orientation of your home and all its rooms, so that you can apply some of the most potent feng shui formulas. You can find out the facing and sitting directions of your home (see Tips 113 and 114,) and once the directions of each room have been established, you can activate the corners to your advantage. Even when you combine different feng shui formulas in your home, the compass directions are essential for accuracy of placing enhancements or cures, or as mentioned previously, to be aware of bad flying star configurations in different areas.

Using a compass to find the orientation of your living space, doors, windows, and furniture is the first step in understanding feng shui. If you can find the center point of your home, position a compass there and get the orientations of your living space from there.

5 the fourth aspect: time dimension feng shui

Time dimension feng shui uses the powerful flying star formula, which refers to numbers of good luck and misfortune which affect and afflict the living space.

So after you have satisfactorily arranged the living space in accordance with all the rules and guidelines to create auspicious energy, it is then necessary to investigate how the luck of any living space can change merely by the passage of time. According to an important school of feng shui practice, every hour, day, month, and year exerts its special essence of invisible, intangible forces. These can bring extreme good fortune or intense misfortune depending on how the time stars affect different corners of your living space. Once again, this aspect of feng shui is well within one's con-

trol. There are easy formulas, which I have condensed into tables (see Chapter 8) so that you will easily see what needs to be done at the start of each month or year in order to avoid misfortunes or to activate some good fortune. This branch of feng shui can often be predictive when you understand the basic formula of calculating the time dimension stars. Once you know the areas that are affected each year, you can apply a cure, if it is necessary, in the appropriate corner so that you will not be affected by the negative energy that will emanate from this space.

This is the annual flying star chart for 2002, the year of the Horse. Note that in this year the lucky sectors which are represented by the lucky numbers 8, 6, and 1 are the northwest, the southeast, and the northeast of the house space or any living space. The most auspicious corner of your rooms in 2002 is therefore the northwest. In that year the unlucky sectors are the north and south, which are both afflicted. North is the place of three killings, or three types of bad luck. South is the place of the illness star and east is the place of the deadly hue, yellow. From this chart you will know instantly which corners to activate and use and which corners to avoid.

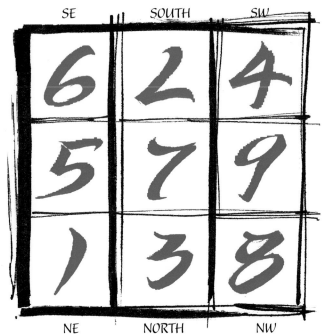

6 introducing the luo pan, or chinese compass

The compass is essential to practice feng shui correctly as orientation is the bedrock of all feng shui analyses and recommendations – the foundation of Chinese feng shui.

Other techniques that deal with enhancing your living space may not use the compass, but it is used by all Chinese feng shui masters in Hong Kong, Taiwan, China, Singapore, and Malaysia, and by those who have migrated to the West and continue to practice genuine Chinese feng shui. Their advice is based on how structures, doors, house locations, contours, and so forth interact with each other in relation to their compass orientation.

The directions indicated by a reliable compass show how chi flows within any environmental space. Every compass direction has a number of attributes that can be related to the physical structures that lie in those directions. This tells us about the quality of chi energy in those areas in terms of space and time.

So if you want to practice genuinely authentic feng shui I have to advise you to get to know and understand the compass. We can start with the Luo Pan, the traditional feng shui compass.

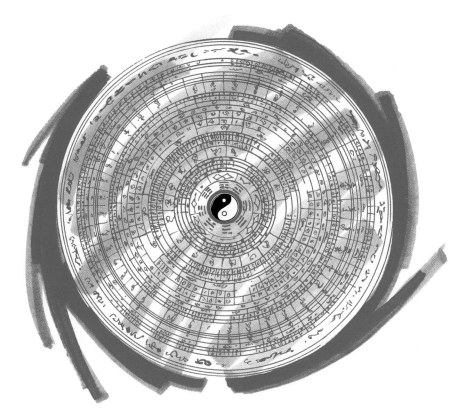

The Luo Pan compass is similar to any Western-style compass, in that it divides directions into 360 degrees around a circle. This is further divided into 8 main directions and 24 sub-directions. These sub-directions are referred to as the 24 mountains, and each mountain measures 15 degrees (360 divided by 24 = 15.) The ring that indicates these 24 mountains is very important, simply because many feng shui formulas use the 24 mountain divisions to express good- and bad-luck orientations.

The three Luo Pans

The traditional Luo Pan is a highly revered work of great craftsmanship. It is always hand made, and its many concentric rings contain the secrets and the formulas of the master who designed it. There are several different types of Luo Pan, but the three most popular and frequently used today are:

1 The Sarn Yuan Luo Pan, which is based on the Three Cycles School. This is also referred to as the Three Period Flying Star Luo Pan.

2 The Sarn Harp Luo Pan, often referred to as the Three Harmony compass. This refers to the harmony between Heaven, Earth, and Man and is reflected in the Man Plate, the Earth Plate, and the Heaven Plate featured on this Luo Pan. These different plates are believed to reflect the three parallel levels of energy flow within the environment, and each takes the north as being 7.5 degrees different from the other. Thus the Earth Plate refers to the magnetic north but the Man and Heaven plates are 7.5 degrees to the left and right of the Earth Plate. So the north referred to in these other plates is not magnetic north.

3 The Sarn He' Luo Pan, which is called the Three Auspicious Happenings School. This looks at the land-forms, mountains, structures, and water that surround any building, and analyzes their good and bad influences based on period numbers, elements, and trigrams.

From the above small description, you can see that the Luo Pan contains a great deal of information. I have repeatedly advised novice practitioners of feng shui that the Luo Pan is not required for those who want to practice feng shui on an amateur basis. It is, however, a good idea to know what this tool is, to use an ordinary compass to take directions, and then refer to a good book to decode the formulas and methods hidden within the Luo Pan.

Please note that the Luo Pan is first and foremost a compass for measuring directions, so its most important part is the magnetic needle, the directional marking in the center. Those who aspire to use a genuine Luo Pan should never compromise on the quality of this central needle. Many of the nuances of good and bad luck depend on accurate compass readings. Always buy a Luo Pan from a feng shui master, who will reveal its code of meanings to you.

7

the western compass in feng shui

Never estimate directions based on where you think the sun rises or sets! This kind of feng shui practice is rarely accurate, and reflects a careless approach, which seldom yields good results.

Consider the compass as an integral part of feng shui. It is, therefore, worthwhile to invest in a good, reliable personal compass. My advice is that you should look for one that has the degrees clearly marked around the outside edge. Compasses that are made with an accompanying ruler are quite useful when you are taking a door direction, because it always ensures that you have placed the compass square to the door.

It is also a good idea to look for a Western-style compass that shows the sub-divisions, or 24 mountains of the main directions. This will then make it extremely easy for you to add extra mileage to your little tool. This is because the 24 subdivisions of compass directions feature in almost all of the popular feng shui formulas, which have survived intact into the 21st century. Knowing how to get your bearings and the orientations of any home correctly and accurately is the vital first step to practicing feng shui.

Types of directions

There are two major types of directions you need to take.

1 You need to know the orientation of your home. Generally, this refers to the direction that your main door faces, but sometimes the main door's facing direction is not the same as the general orientation of the house. In such situations, use your compass and take both these directions, then refer to Tips 9 and 10 for further analysis. Also, those of you who live in apartments should take the direction of both the entrance into the apartment building and entrance door into your apartment.

2 You need to get the orientation of the inside of your home. So read the compass from the center of the house (see Tip 11.)

Hold a compass flat or place on a flat surface for accurate readings.

Compass checklist

- Always take directions holding the compass perfectly flat on your palm, as this will ensure a more accurate reading.

- Make allowances for your compass being affected by metallic or electrical energy fields, so take directions three times.

- Try to take directions at waist level for a better chi reading.

- Always have a floor plan nearby so you can mark in the directions immediately. This leaves less room for error.

8 how to take compass directions

A good, solid compass will always have a dial that shows the degrees of all the eight directions, as well as the 24 subdivisions of the directions.

Before you can practice feng shui, you must familiarize yourself thoroughly with your compass. You should learn to read the directions so that you can instantly get the orientation of any place. If you do not get this orientation correctly measured out, it is really not possible to practice authentic Chinese feng shui.

Use a compass that has the degrees of the directions clearly marked.

Compass points

- A single compass point is represented by 360 degrees.

- Each of the four cardinal and four secondary directions occupies an angle of 45 degrees. Thus 45 multiplied by 8 makes 360 degrees. So when we extend the space from

any single point occupied by any of the eight directions, the space we will be referring to is that which is contained within a 45-degree angle. You can see this if you consider each of the directions to be like a slice taken from a round pie – therefore, this method of reading the compass and identifying space is called the Pie Chart method. The main directions are north, south, east, and west. The secondary directions are northeast, northwest, southeast, and southwest. Each of these directions occupies an angle of 45 degrees extended out from any single point of reference.

- Each of these 8 directions can be further subdivided into three, so each 45-degree angle can be subdivided into three 15-degree parts. These subdivisions are usually referred to as the mountains and, because there are a total of 24 subdivisions resulting from the 8 directions, there are said to be 24 mountains in the compass. Therefore, the 24 mountains refer to 15-degree subdivisions of the compass.

Take note that while the illustrations in this and all my feng shui books show the direction south at the top of any compass, this does not mean that south is on top when you are taking the directions of your home. You need the compass to find out where the south is in your home. You need the compass to point it out to you! It is the same with all the other directions and sub-directions.

9 how to align a compass correctly

A key skill in feng shui is learning to align a compass correctly so that the direction indicated on the compass face shows a correct reading of the direction.

This is because the whole science of feng shui is predicated on the way direction energy moves and interacts within any given space.

It is useful to know that feng shui theory has much of its roots intertwined with the Taoist view of the Universe and of existence. Hence, the flow of chi energy is measured both within a microcosm as well as encompassing the entire macrocosm of space. It is up to us to delineate and define the space we are working with; we need to take the orientations of that space and also know the impact of the space that falls outside this boundary.

In feng shui language, this is referred to as the big tai chi – the bigger surrounding space – and the small tai chi, which can mean the space of the entire home, the space of the entire apartment building, or the space of the individual whole apartment. It can also mean the space of individual rooms. Understanding this concept of big and small tai chi opens up huge possibilities in applying and interpreting formulas. However, it also has implications when it comes to delineating compass sectors of rooms and homes.

What to do about varying readings

Localized accuracy is an important factor. This means learning to align the compass for the whole apartment or home, and then repeating it locally

Use a ruler to make sure your compass is accurately aligned with a door or wall.

in each of the individual rooms for more accurate readings. It should not come as a surprise that every room would show some small variations in the readings of directions. In such cases, go with the localized reading, as this gives you the correct energy directions of the particular space being investigated.

When the difference in orientation and direction exceeds 15 degrees as you move from room to room, this could indicate some quite severe imbalance of the energy within a room or home. This is often a clue that the furniture arrangement and placement of decorative items is out of sync with the natural flow of energy there. It is then advisable to make some changes to the placement and arrangement of room furniture. One simple and effective method to get the balance right is to move the furniture around until the variation in readings falls below 5 degrees.

10 determining the general direction of your home

When you start using your compass you may be faced with a dilemma about how you can best work out the correct orientation of your home.

Now that you know how to read the compass correctly and accurately, it is useful to clarify some of the points of confusion you will meet up with in the course of analyzing the personal feng shui of your own space, and also when you try to apply the Tips dealt with later in this book.

There can be quite a number of problem areas in feng shui; one of the more confusing issues facing the novice practitioner is how to determine the correct orientation of a home. Exactly which direction should we take if we are to determine the facing direction of a home? It is easy enough when a home is a perfect regular shape and the main door faces the same direction as the general orientation of the home itself – then there is no room for doubt whatsoever. But what if the door

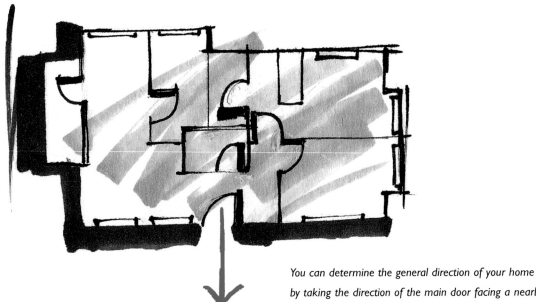

Main door direction

You can determine the general direction of your home by taking the direction of the main door facing a nearby road, or the door of the home that is most frequently used by the family. However, if you cannot decide which to use, walk around the house several times and feel exactly where maximum yang energy is coming from. Only then can you feel confident that the orientation you have taken is correct.

When you want to get the orientation of your home, start at the main door. Stand there and look out; the direction you are facing directly in front is the facing direction and this is generally regarded as the orientation of your home.

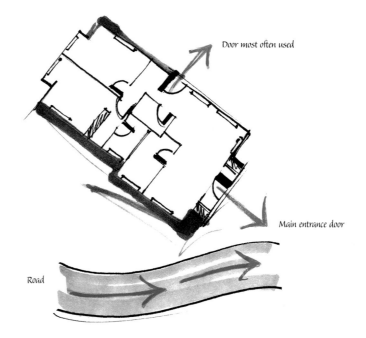

Door most often used

Main entrance door

Road

faces one direction, and the house is oriented to another direction? Which then is the direction to take for feng shui analysis and reference?

Finding a solution can be particularly troublesome, because different masters can recommend different approaches. So here are three important alternatives to consider when you are determining any orientations.

Of the three alternative orientations, I use my judgement on the basis of on-site investigation. All are feasible and have certain respectability. I personally know different masters who use all three different options based on their perception of the house being investigated, and all use this with some success. So my advice is to use your own judgement after duly considering each of the three options. Please also note that, in feng shui, homes that have a clearly defined main door have the best potential for enjoying continuous good fortune. Homes that lack this cause chi flow to be uncertain and unstable, thereby creating the cause of uncertain luck.

Three ways to take directions

1 Take the direction that is indicated by the main door, i.e. when you are standing at the largest entrance door looking out. Determine the direction that this door faces. This is one direction that can qualify as the main direction for you to use.

2 Take the direction that is indicated by the main road outside your house. This is the direction from which maximum yang energy comes into the home. So, if the house is oriented towards a road, take this as the facing orientation of the house, even if the main door itself actually faces another direction.

3 Take the direction of the door that is the most frequently used by the members of the family. This is because one definition of the main door is that which is most frequently used. As the main door is said to represent the "mouth" of the home, this is another correct orientation to take.

11 finding the orientation of interior space

Another common problem faced by novice practitioners, especially those who have read different books on the subject, is how to determine the general orientation of the inside of the home.

When you are advised to activate a specific corner of your home confusion arises when the corner is indicated by its direction. For instance, if you are asked to activate the north in order to energize your career luck, this immediately begs a whole series of questions. How do you determine the north corner? Does this mean the north corner of the entire home? And, if so, what if the north corner is missing? and so on.

Taking these practical dilemmas one at a time, the first matter to be resolved is to learn to determine the orientations of the home so you can identify the eight compass "corners" on your floor plan. To do this correctly, once again you will need to take directions with a compass. In authentic feng shui, orientations always require the compass and they are never determined by the location of the main door. Orientations should never be calculated according to the main door having a fixed direction. I have received thousands of emails asking about this, mainly because some practitioners trained in another method of feng shui use this method. In Chinese feng shui, this is not the way to do it.

Take compass directions inside the main door and again a few feet further inside.

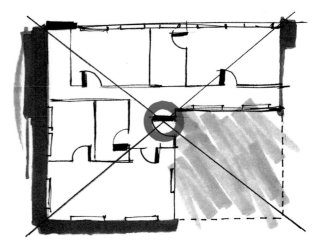

Take a third compass direction from the center of your home. If your home is an irregular shape, mark in missing areas on your floor plan and draw diagonal lines (as shown) to find its center.

12 understanding the lo shu square

The next step in practical feng shui is to familiarize yourself with one of the most important, and effective, feng shui symbols that can be used on your floor plan.

This is the Lo Shu Square, which is a nine-sector grid, each containing a number from 1 to 9. The numbers are arranged in the grid so that when any three numbers are added, they add up to 15, which is also the number of days it takes the moon to grow from a new moon to a full moon, and vice versa. The Chinese Taoist scholars regard the Lo Shu as a magic square and believe that it provides the key to unlocking many of the secrets of feng shui's other important symbol, the eight-sided Pa Kua (see Tips 14 and 15.)

According to legend, the magical Lo Shu Square of numbers was carried on the back of the celestial tortoise and brought to the attention of the Chinese Emperor, Fu Hsi. So today, the tortoise is revered as an auspicious creature whose body and shell are said to conceal special design motifs that contain all the secrets contained in heaven and earth.

I started writing books about feng shui soon after I picked up the shell of a dead turtle that had been washed up on the shore on a seaside vacation trip to Pangkor Island with my family. That was in 1992. At that time I failed to note the significance of that omen, and although I brought the shell back home, I discarded it soon afterwards. I only realized the symbolism while one day meditating by my pond where my pet terrapins lived (terrapins are domestic tortoises and turtles are the marine relations of the freshwater tortoise.) It was while I observed the patterns on the back of these playful creatures that the significance of that symbolic find struck me.

Later, as you go deeper into your practice of feng shui, you will discover how important and clever the Lo Shu Square of numbers is when it comes to both hiding and revealing the secrets of formula and compass feng shui. For now, just familiarize yourself with the Lo Shu Square, its numbers and directions, and how it can be used to demarcate the layout of your floor plan.

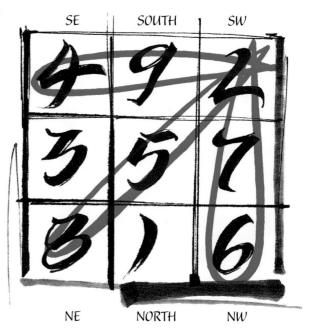

13 placing the lo shu square over a floor plan

Now you have learnt the basics about the importance of the Lo Shu Square, you can experiment with placing it over your home's floor plan.

While this is easy enough to do if the layout of your home is a perfect square, unfortunately this is seldom the case – most homes do have an irregular layout.

Modern homes are rarely, if ever, perfectly square or rectangular. In hallways or in the rooms there will be missing corners and protruding corners, and sometimes the shapes are so irregular that even the real chi that enters gets confused by the flow which is created by the unusual shape of the home.

You also need to know whether to include or exclude portions of the home that appear to protrude. Also, what about including areas occupied by garages, patios, decks, or verandas? In view of the great many variations of house plans and shapes, superimposing the nine-sector grid is therefore something of a challenge to those unfamiliar with feng shui applications. Here are a few specific guidelines that I have put together, based on my experience and advice given to me by practicing feng shui masters.

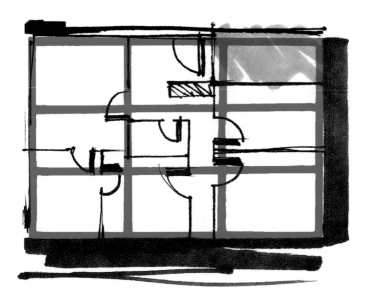

To superimpose the Lo Shu Square over an irregular-shaped home, extend the missing areas on your floor plan. When you overlay the square you will see which area of it you are missing. Here, the southwest is missing, which is associated with love and relationships.

Lo Shu lore

- For interiors in both houses and apartments, the Lo Shu Square should be superimposed onto all the built-up areas that share a roof mass. This means that for apartments you should first superimpose the Square onto the whole building, then apply it to the apartment space itself. This will give a much more accurate assessment of the apartment's feng shui and its suitability for a resident.

- When there is more than one level, each level should be treated separately, since different floors usually have different areas and dimensions.

- When the floor space is irregular, some masters superimpose two different Lo Shu Squares. Personally, I prefer to use one grid and treat areas that are empty as missing corners.

- When a floor plan is narrow and deep or broad and shallow, some masters look at the way the rooms in the home have been arranged and use a six-grid Lo Shu instead of the traditional nine-grid Lo Shu. This means dropping the center grids. I prefer to continue using the nine-grid Lo Shu, with the demarcated sectors equally worked out in terms of floor area. Therefore, in effect, the Lo Shu Square can be stretched vertically or horizontally.

Superimposing the Lo Shu onto a floor plan is the most practical method of demarcating sectors within the home. This enables the practitioner to identify the different corners for purposes of applying the different formulas, and also energize the corner according to the Elements that are allocated to each of the sectors. In short, superimposing the grid enables you to start understanding the energy of your space and take action to enhance it.

For regular floor plans, the Lo Shu Square should fit proportionally over the available space. Here, the rectangular shape of the individual squares reflects the overall shape of the floor plan.

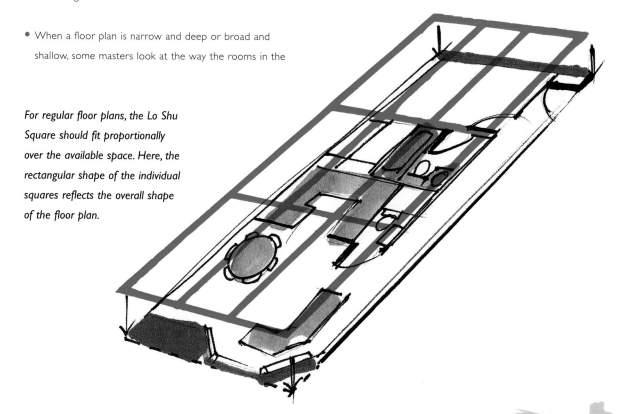

14 understanding the two pa kuas

The Pa Kua is an eight-sided symbol which signifies many of the secrets of feng shui. It is a special tool that is a central part of feng shui practice. It can be used for assessment or protection.

Each of the eight sides of the Pa Kua has several associations, including a direction, an element, a member of the family, and an organ.

Most significantly, on each side of the Pa Kua is one of the eight root trigrams of the *I Ching*. How these trigrams are placed around the different sides of the Pa Kua determines what kind of Pa Kua it is. There are two arrangements to these trigrams and therefore there are two kinds of Pa Kua: the Yin Pa Kua and the Yang Pa Kua.

The Yin Pa Kua

Here the trigrams are arranged in what is described as a cyclical pattern, where the trigrams are arranged as pairs of opposites. This arrangement is generally referred to as the Early Heaven Arrangement of trigrams. The most important trigram, Ch'ien, which represents heaven and the patriarch, is placed in the south and directly opposite in the north is the trigram that represents the matriarch, the trigram K'un. These two are the ultimate yang and yin trigrams respectively. So there is nothing more yang than Ch'ien, and there is nothing more yin than K'un. The arrangement of the trigrams in the Yin Pa Kua is said to possess intrinsic power that can control shar chi, or killing energy. Thus this is the arrangement that is placed round the Pa Kua used for deflecting the poison

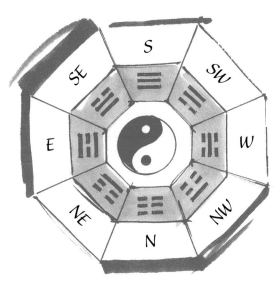

The Yin Pa Kua's *arrangement of trigrams create protective yin energy when placed outside the home.*

arrows of straight roads, T-junctions, and other harmful structures. The Yin Pa Kua is essentially a remedy tool in feng shui practice.

It should never be displayed or hung anywhere inside the home. It should not be used to counter poison arrows that are present inside the home. In destroying the shar chi of the poison arrow, it will also harm residents who inadvertently get hit by the Pa Kua. I stress this very strenuously as I am aware of people masquerading as feng shui masters who sell Pa Kua mirrors and recommend they be hung inside the home. Please don't do this, as it is very dangerous.

15 understanding the yang pa kua

This is the diagnostic Pa Kua that is used to analyze the feng shui and chi flow of all the rooms contained in homes and offices.

The arrangement of the trigrams in this Pa Kua is the Later Heaven Arrangement, and here they reflect the premise that the relationship between the opposites of the Early Heaven Arrangement has given way to changes. The philosophy behind this Pa Kua is the inevitability of change. So now the trigram that is placed in the south is no longer Ch'ien but is instead the trigram Li, and the trigram in the north is no longer K'un, but Kan. The ultimate yang and yin trigrams are now placed in the northwest and southwest respectively.

Placement of the trigrams

It is when you spend a little time taking note of the arrangement of trigrams and their placement around this Yang Pa Kua that you begin to really understand the fundamental basis of feng shui practice. For now it is sufficient to know that we use the Yang Pa Kua for analysis for our feng shui practice, and not the Yin Pa Kua, which is more suitable for yin dwellings, or graveyards. So to practice feng shui, learn the attributes of each of the sides of the Yang Pa Kua.

The Pa Kua contains six rings that give different information to the feng shui practitioner (see Tip 16.) One ring gives the life aspiration, for example career prospects or recognition and

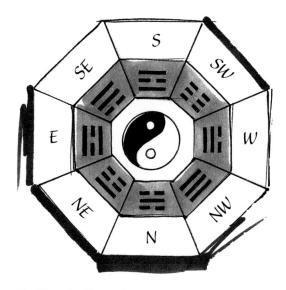

The Yang Pa Kua is the one that is used in feng shui analysis. The difference between this and the Yin Pa Kua is the way the trigrams have been placed. The arrangement of trigrams here is known as the Later Heaven Arrangement. This reflects the essence of yang feng shui. It reflects the cyclical nature of energy and shows how this can be activated to create and accumulate quantities of precious yang energy. It is this yang energy that brings life, activity, success, and joyousness to living spaces. In advanced feng shui work, both the Pa Kuas are combined to analyze the landforms around the home.

fame; the second the compass direction; the third the color of the Element; the fourth the Element, such as Water or Fire; the fifth the trigram; and the sixth the trigram character itself.

16

how to use the yang pa kua in feng shui practice

Now we come to the first and easiest way to practice feng shui. The Pa Kua has many different rings with varying attributes to enhance your home.

I call this the Eight Aspirations of Mankind method as signified by the eight root trigrams of the *I Ching* that are placed around the eight-sided Pa Kua. Note that each side represents one direction. So as there are eight sides, all the eight directions of the compass around a central point are accounted for.

From the preceding pages we have already learned how to take directions and how to identify the different directions and sectors of the home. Now we will need to analyze the Yang Pa Kua in order to transfer the attributes of each of the eight sides of the Pa Kua onto your home and to do this in such a way that the quality of the chi in each sector of your home is enhanced with preliminary, but extremely fundamental, feng shui techniques.

First study the many layers of meanings associated with each of the eight different sides of the Yang Pa Kua shown here. Note that every direction sector contains different attributes that offer clues to how that part of any living space can be activated, energized,

and enhanced. The energy of each sector also has a yin or a yang aspect and every sector is representative of the Element energy assigned to that sector under this arrangement of the trigrams. In the following pages the practical implications of each of the layers shown in the Pa Kua will be explained. Later, when we learn to go deeper and start to use the formulas of feng shui, the attributes of the directions as shown in the Pa Kua will take on even deeper and greater significance, so do spend some time studying these attributes.

From the Yang Pa Kua may be derived many rings of characteristics and element symbolism that give meaning to compass sectors.

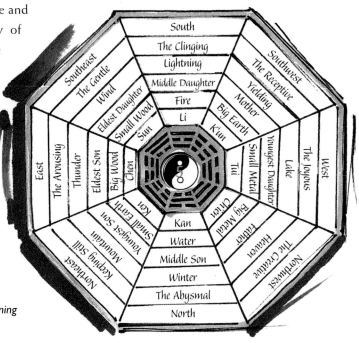

17 assess the pa kua sectors separately

Each home sector should be carefully assessed to see if there are imbalances in the energy there that should be corrected using the attributes of the Pa Kua.

Using the Pa Kua highlights the effects of missing and protruding corners, which can be good or bad depending on how they impact on the personalized feng shui of residents. Detailed examination of the sectors also shows the effect of shapes, colors, and room usage on the overall luck of the family.

Here the way you assess the sectors depends on whether you use the Lo Shu method or the Pie Chart method. The space covered under the two methods differs quite considerably. If you examine

The Pie Chart Method

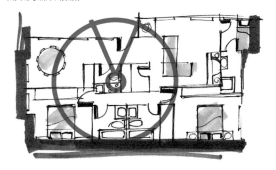

The Lo Shu Method

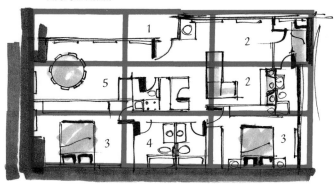

the two methods used on the floor plans below, you will see how the rooms and corners of rooms deemed to fall into different directions of the compass sectors differ quite considerably. If you are unsure which method to use you might want to follow my example and do away with the Pie Chart method completely. I have always used the Lo Shu Square method to demarcate rooms as I find this to be the most practical.

In addition, readers may be interested to know that the Lo Shu numbers actually make up the base upon which many of the most powerful formulas of feng shui are formulated. Secondly, since most rooms of most houses are either square or rectangular, using the grid method is much easier from a practical viewpoint. Some of you may find that certain rooms fall into two, or even three, different sectors. In such cases, the conventional wisdom to which many feng shui masters of repute subscribe is to follow the attributes indicated by the largest floor area covered.

1. The entrance is in the north sector.
2. The living room is in the east and northeast, which protrudes so the east and northeast are emphasized.
3. Bedrooms are in the southeast and southwest.
4. Bathrooms and toilets are in the south.
5. The dining room is in the west.

18 the eight directions and the five elements

Probably the most significant thing to commit to memory regarding the eight directions is the element that is associated with each of the directions.

In fact the importance of the Five Elements – Earth, Metal, Water, Wood, and Fire – pervades so much of feng shui practice that those most knowledgeable about the interpretation of Elements are regarded as the best feng shui masters in the world. Practitioners of this calibre are those whose knowledge of the Elements is so profound that they can just look at a building and immediately draw potent signals from the Elements there that will tell them about its luck.

So, to get the most out of the practice, you need to learn which Element is associated with which direction. With this understanding, you can bring good feelings and good chi into your home, by ensuring the balance and harmony of elements within each of the sectors. The simple Pa Kua here shows which Element is assigned to each of the directions based on what is referred to as the Earth plate of the compass. Please note that in feng shui practice there are three plates – the Heaven plate, the Earth plate, and the Man plate. In advanced feng shui, all three plates are factored into the practice and this reflects the harmony between Heaven, Earth, and Man. Each of these plates uses a different north, and in the Earth plate, the north is the magnetic north. The north referred to in the other plates is not the magnetic north. Beginners need to use only the Earth plate as the reference point, but it is useful to know

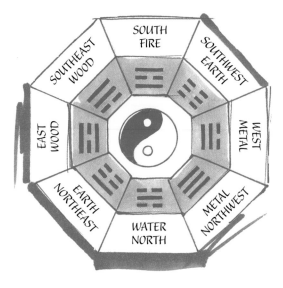

Each direction is associated with an element: Fire, Earth, Metal, Water, or Wood.

about the other plates since the allocation of the Five Elements to each of the directions in the other plates is not the same. When you know this you will not be confused when you find Elements being assigned to directions other than those here.

Yang Elements

In general feng shui practice we apply the Elements that are allocated according to the Yang Pa Kua (illustrated here.) Take note of which Element is represented in each of the eight directions.

19

the eight directions and their meanings

The eight primary trigrams that are the roots of the *I Ching*'s 64 hexagrams are powerful symbols that are combinations of three straight lines that are either broken or unbroken.

These trigrams collectively symbolize a trinity of world principles that are recognized as the Subject (Man,) the Object having form (Earth,) and the Content (Heaven.) Every trigram has multiple sets of meanings, symbols, and connotations. These are arranged around the eight sides of the octagonal-shaped Pa Kua in two recognized sequences from which are derived a great deal of meanings that can be used very effectively by a feng shui practitioner.

In fact, extensive references are frequently made to the trigrams because their meanings offer valuable clues to the practitioner in that, not only do the trigrams each correspond to the cardinal points and compass directions, but they also represent one of the Elements. This is expressed either as a "soft" or a "dark" aspect, which possesses either a yin and yang connotation, and also stands for a specific member of the family. For yang homes (i.e. the dwellings of the living) the meaning derived from the trigram sequences offers valuable insights into how each of the directions can have far-reaching effects on the different aspects of luck for all the residents of a dwelling.

So the meanings of the trigrams as laid out in the Yang Pa Kua indicate that each direction symbolizes different luck. To strengthen the luck of the sectors, clever enhancement of the Element and its relevant sector is needed. See the list opposite.

- South affects recognition luck. When enhanced brings honor, fame, and a good reputation. When afflicted, brings shame, disgrace, and at its worse could lead to imprisonment.

- North stands for success at work. When enhanced, success comes easily. When afflicted, blocks and obstacles appear constantly that prevent success from happening.

- East brings good fortune to the sons of the family and creates excellent descendants' luck when properly activated.

- Southeast brings growth, expansion, and wealth. When afflicted, causes financial loss and shrinkage of assets. Very sensitive to the physical activators placed here. When afflicted, sons suffer and family harmony is affected.

- West brings good health; if afflicted, affects family's women.

- Southwest represents the luck of the matriarch. When afflicted, relationships suffer and marriage luck is curtailed. When strengthened, brings marriage happiness.

- Northeast brings scholarly and literary luck. When activated this sector brings excellent luck.

- Northwest affects the family patriarch and brings influence, patronage, and power to the residents. When afflicted, causes grievous harm to the family head.

20 the eight directions and the family

Another dimension of Pa Kua feng shui analysis focuses on the eight trigrams and the luck associated with different family members: the father, mother, three sons, and three daughters.

The feng shui of any home should always include an investigation of sectors that represent important family members, such as the father and mother. You need to ensure that their trigram corners are not afflicted in any way and, if they are, take immediate remedial measures. Read the associations below and consider them carefully.

The father is in the northwest

In the northwest is the trigram Ch'ien, the most powerful and important of the eight trigrams, because it represents the father. The wellbeing, prosperity, and status of the household depend upon how auspicious this corner of the house is. It is very worthwhile to ensure that the northwest part of the home or the living room is not made inauspicious in any way, either due to the presence of toilets, sharp angular objects, wrong colors, or a lack of strong yang, or male, energy. Counter all these afflictions by dissolving or blocking everything that may be harmful here. When the northwest of any home is afflicted or is missing, it indicates a weak, or non-existent, patriarch. The whole family suffers, so place a bright light inside northwest toilets to counter the negative effect, and keep Metal-element energy strong by hanging windchimes and having a white color scheme.

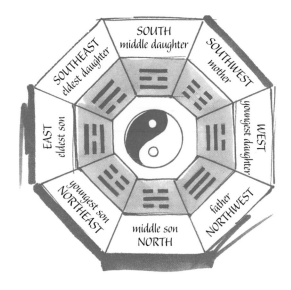

Each of the eight directions on the Yang Pa Kua is associated with a member of the family. Check out the areas of your home that represent each person. Removing afflictions in these areas can help improve their luck.

The mother is in the southwest

In the southwest is the equally important trigram K'un, which is the archetype of the maternal, or mother earth. This corner trigram, represented by three broken yin lines, symbolizes nurturing and yielding. It has strong yin power and signifies relationships, marriage, and the wellbeing of the family. This corner also affects the luck of the women of the house, so it should really not be afflicted in anyway. Toilets here cause obstacles to

The Eight Primary Trigrams

The eight trigrams have yin and yang properties. Note that Ch'ien, for the father, has three unbroken lines denoting maximum yang, or male, energy. K'un is the opposite, meaning maximum female, or yin, energy.

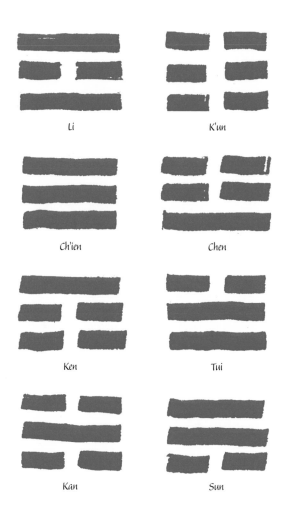

Li

K'un

Ch'ien

Chen

Ken

Tui

Kan

Sun

marriage happiness for daughters. You can cure this affliction by painting the door a bright red on the outside, or place a tall plant inside the toilet. The matriarch of the family will suffer when the southwest is afflicted, so always make sure that you do something. When the southwest is protected in this way, all the most noble qualities of motherhood will be activated, bringing good fortune for the family.

The eldest son is in the east

The third important location to pay careful attention to is the east, where the ruling trigram is Chen, which embodies the spirit of the first male descendant. When this corner is afflicted the eldest son is at risk. When it is made auspicious he shines brightly, bringing honor to the family. If a toilet occupies this area, hang a windchime there. If the east is missing, place a large plant close to the missing area to encourage fortunate chi for the eldest son.

The eldest daughter is in the southeast

In the southeast resides the trigram Sun, which embodies the spirit of the eldest daughter. This is the corner that brings prosperity. Again, this corner should be protected and not missing.

Locations of younger children

• The north (trigram Kan) represents the middle son of the family.

• The south (trigram Li) signifies the middle daughter.

• The northeast (trigram Ken) is the place of the youngest son.

• The west (trigram Tui) is the place of the youngest daughter, who brings joy.

21 the eight directions and the body

Feng shui orientations in the home and the smooth flow of chi in the various sectors also affect the wellbeing and health of residents.

Depending on how each of the home sectors are afflicted, specific problems can develop that affect the parts of the body symbolized by the different directions. These are based on the trigrams of the sector and their Elements.

Internal parts of the body are affected when the Elements of the home are weak and afflicted. So when the Fire sector (south) is negatively afflicted, either by physical disharmony caused by furniture placement, bad shapes, or wrong conflicting colors, or due to bad flying stars (formula feng shui), then the internal organ associated with the Fire Element will cause problems for the resident staying in the south. So understanding the relationship between the organs of the body and the Elements in accordance with the eight directions will add great breadth to your feng shui practice.

The heart and small intestine is of the Fire Element, the kidneys are of the Water Element, the lungs and colon are of the Metal Element, the liver is of the Wood Element, and the spleen and the stomach are of the Earth Element. This means that when the north is afflicted, residents sleeping there who are unwell may have kidney or bladder problems. When the east and southeast manifest health problems, those staying there may have liver or gall bladder-related ailments. Those staying in Earth sectors – the southwest and northeast – are vulnerable to stomach or spleen disorders.

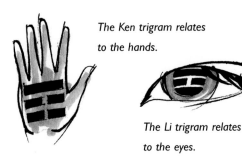

The Ken trigram relates to the hands.

The Li trigram relates to the eyes.

The orientations within the home are also associated with body parts. Thus the northwest is associated with the head. So, for example, when the northwest is negatively affected, residents sleeping there may suffer from headaches and other disorders associated with the head. Using the same analysis, below is a summary of the body parts affected in accordance with afflicted sectors of the home.

Feng shui body language

- The north (trigram Kan): Ears
- The southwest (trigram K'un): Illness affects the older women, and the nose
- The east (trigram Chen): Feet and the hair
- The southeast (trigram Sun): Buttock and neck pain
- The west (trigram Tui): Mouth
- The northeast (trigram Ken): Hands and fingers
- The south (trigram Li): Eyes
- The northwest (trigram Ch'ien): Head

22 the eight substances indicated by the trigrams

There is a close relationship between different feng shui formulae and the trigrams of the Pa Kua. Knowing the eight substances associated with each trigram fosters valuable insights into them.

The eight substances and their trigram origins and compass directions are summarized here.

Fire links to the trigram Li in the south. This substance is also one of the Five Elements. This trigram symbolizes the brightness of fire and the dazzle of the sun. It stands for glory; the applause of the masses. Li also suggests activity and heat. The symbolism of the Fire substance is that of a great man who perpetuates the light by rising to prominence. The color of Li is red, the bright red that suggests celebrations and happy occasions. To benefit from the chi of the south, activate Fire in this corner.

Heaven is associated with leadership, massive yang forces, and power. The trigram is Ch'ien and the direction is northwest, the place of the patriarch. To attract the luck of heaven, activate with gold energy simulated by metal objects. To produce good feng shui for the father, place a pile of polished decorative stones in the northwest corner. Spray gold paint on the stones to simulate gold. This is a good technique, as the Element of the northwest is Big Metal, and in feng shui terms, metal is like gold. The pile of stones represents the Earth Element in which gold is found. The energies created are in harmonious balance.

Earth and Mountain These down-to-earth, grounding substances are represented by the powerful K'un and Ken trigrams. These substances of

Left: Gold stones in the northwest create patriarch luck.
Right: Fish in the north of the living room bring wealth luck.

the Earth Element stand for matriarchal wisdom forces that signifies real strength, sustenance, and family-related happiness. A pile of boulders here is excellent, but do not exhaust the Earth energy by spraying gold. A crystal cluster is also excellent. The directions are southwest and northeast.

Water is the substance of power and wealth. It is a substance that can bring great prosperity or hardship and suffering, so the water chi must be harnessed carefully. It has a double-edged effect: placed in the north, water brings luck, but differentiate between the flow of water and actual placement of water. It is easier to work with water features than to harness luck from water flow, so a fish tank in the north corner of the living room, for example, is always good and always beneficial.

The other three substances are symbolized by the lake, thunder, and wind. These align with the trigrams in the west, east, and southeast. Paintings and decorative objects give life to the energies of these substances.

23 the yin and yang of the four cardinal directions

In feng shui practice, it is helpful to develop sensitivity to yin and yang energies. This understanding means the difference between success and failure when placing all your feng shui enhancers.

In a similar way to placing the final piece in the feng shui jigsaw, yin and yang energy makes the picture whole and complete. So understanding its manifestations is a crucial starting point in developing feng shui instincts.

The Chinese believe that yin and yang forces give existence to each other. So, yin is passive, darkness, night, cold, quiet, and stillness; yang, on the other hand, is positive, daylight, brightness, warmth, heat, sounds, and activity. They cannot exist without the other, so without the yin of cold there is no yang warmth, and without yang sunshine, there can be no yin moonlight! Another attribute of the yin-yang cosmology is that one contains the seed of the other. So in yang there must always be a little bit of yin, and vice versa, so that when there is an excess of either, the space affected is said to be unbalanced and not in harmony. When such a situation occurs, it is felt that there just cannot be any good luck.

So in feng shui, yin-yang balance requires the simultaneous presence of both the forces. However, because we are dealing with life energy when we speak of yang feng shui, it is vital that the environment must always have yang energy and yet should never be too yin. Maintaining this very delicate balance between the two forces is really the essence of feng shui practice – what it is essentially all about.

Yin and yang for male and female

The yin and yang aspects of directions are usually indicated by the + and − signs; plus and minus, positive and negative. So every one of the eight directions contains both yin and yang aspects. In the cardinal directions north, south, east, and west, there is more yin than yang, but this signifies strong yang and weak yin. Indeed, this situation indicates a young, emerging, and vibrant yang. The distribution of yin and yang forces for all the four cardinal directions is therefore yang, yin yin or plus minus minus in the first, second, and third sub-directions of each sector.

So, for example, in the north there is north 1, north 2, and north 3; north 1 is yang, and north 2 and 3 are yin. So males should always choose north 2 and north 3 as their most suitable north directions, while females should always select north 1 as their auspicious northerly direction. When you do this, you will find that it helps to cement the yin and yang presence, which then strengthens the balance that brings you success in your life and good fortune.

Always take note of this particular fine point when working with your directions and the corners of you home as, by using this method, you will find this is the optimum way of ensuring that your feng shui will work for you.

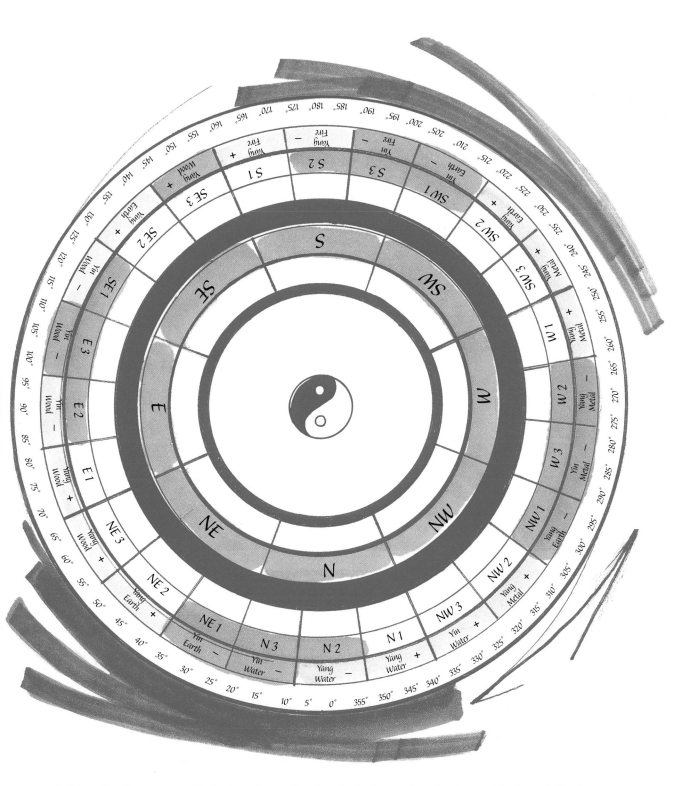

A Chinese Luo Pan compass with the yin and yang allocations for the four cardinal directions and the four sub-directions.

24

the yin and yang of the secondary four directions

The secondary directions of the compass also contain both yin and yang aspects. As for the four cardinal directions, it is very important to study their attributes.

In the secondary directions, the yin and yang aspects are also signified by the + and − signs.

Once again, there are plus and minus sub-directions as well as positive and negative connotations to the directions. But here in the northeast, southeast, northwest, and southwest (see the compass in Tip 23,) there is more yang than yin energy. This situation signifies a strong yin and weak yang. It indicates a young, emerging, and vibrant yin, while yang has grown old and is now tired. The distribution of yin and yang forces for all four secondary directions is therefore yin-yang-yang, or minus-plus-plus in the first, second, and third sub-directions of each sector. So, for example, in the southwest sector, there is southwest 1, southwest 2, and southwest 3. Southwest 1 is yin and southwest 2 and 3 are yang. So males should choose southwest 1 as their most suitable southwest directions, while females should select southwest 2 or 3 as their auspicious southwest direction.

This seals the yin and yang presence, which will, in turn, strengthen the balance that brings you good feng shui. Do not forget to take note of this particular fine point when you are working with your directions and the corners of you home, and especially when you are practicing the personalized directions of Eight Mansions feng shui (see Chapter 4.)

This is truly an important fine point that ensures success for you in your feng shui work. Shown on the previous page in Tip 23 is an illustration of the compass directions with the sub-directions marked in and also the yin and yang sub-directions clearly depicted. These sub-directions are referred to by advanced feng shui practitioners as the 24 mountains, which themselves contain further keys to the unlocking of advanced feng shui formulas. Now you know that this term merely refers to the three subsections of the eight compass directions.

2

feng shui

makeovers

for interiors

25

regularize the shape of your floor plan

The shape and structure of every piece of furniture and decorative item inside the living space of any home has either good or bad feng shui implications.

The basic principles concerning auspicious or inauspicious shapes are based on: whether the shapes are regular or irregular, whether there are missing or protruding corners, the Element attribute of the shape itself, and whether the shape resembles a lucky or hostile symbol.

Auspicious shapes

These are a perfect square or rectangular, whether flat to show the layout of rooms, or standing to represent the vertical shape of buildings or furniture. These are the most regular shapes, and are the easiest to work with to produce good feng shui.

Inauspicious or difficult shapes

These are believed to create imbalances and an uncertain flow of chi. Layouts where the room is

an odd shape often cause the luck of the occupants to be uncertain and unstable. To improve fortunes, such shapes should be regularized with clever placement of furniture, and using floor and wall colors and lighting to create different perspectives. Always strive to regularize the appearance of any room with its interior decoration as it will always make it more auspicious.

Irregular shapes

These give rise to missing corners and will always create problems in interior feng shui. The severity of the problem depends on which corner is missing. So if you divide your home layout into nine equal grids (see Tip 13) and then check the compass direction of each of the grids you will be able to identify the compass direction represented by the missing corner.

Auspicious shapes

Inauspicious shapes

26 auspicious shapes for home interiors

When I refer to shapes, I mean the shape of the layout of the entire house as well as the shape of individual rooms and the walls inside each room.

It is always preferable to opt for a regular symmetrical shape. In feng shui terms anything that is irregular or asymmetrical always indicates that something is missing or is incomplete. So a full square is always a better shape than a narrow version of one. A full circle is always better than a half circle, and for this reason bay windows are seldom encouraged as good feng shui. Small irregularities in the corners of rooms are equally discouraged. The Pa Kua (or eight-sided shape), the diagnostic tool used in feng shui, is also considered a very auspicious shape especially when it is used for dining and coffee tables.

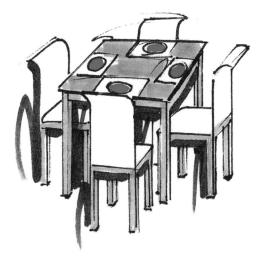

Square-shaped dining tables are excellent for a small family. The shape suggests perfect balance and grounded symmetry creating easy, harmonious relationships.

Colour and shape

Walls should always be painted to make the regularity of their shape stand out.

Here are some guidelines for using shape and color to bring family harmony and success. Rectangular walls which are taller rather than broader (without appearing incomplete) are particularly good in the east and southeast corners as this shape signifies growth and success. This is the shape of the Wood Element and Wood suggests the season of spring, a time of growth.

Perfectly square shapes, which belong to the Earth Element, are ideal for the dining room and

The Pa Kua-shaped dining table is superb for a family with three generations living together. You can allocate the chairs according to each person's best directions.

the dining table since not only does this reflect the stability of grounding energy, but Earth also stands for the mother. The energy of the square shape is very balanced and is very auspicious for family harmony.

Round shapes denote the Metal Element and these are suitable for the west and northwest areas. It is a good idea to create a perfect round patch with clever paintwork techniques on any northwest wall so that you create auspicious luck for the patriarch of the family. Paint it gold for added radiance and additional good luck symbolism. Do not make the shape too large as the round shape can be overpowering for residential homes. In large corporate offices, however, they are ideal when featured in the northwest.

Linking to Elements

On the north walls of living and dining rooms you can use color to create the wavy shape of its Element Water. This will create good career luck for the residents. Cover the bottom half of the wall with this shape to enhance the grounding nature of water. The result will help bring better recognition at work and also enhanced promotion opportunities for you.

In terms of shapes, it is a good idea to avoid using the Fire Element shape. The fire shape is triangular and this is generally considered as inauspicious and unsuitable for home interiors, mainly because fire inside the home can be one of the signs of danger. Too much of the Fire Element will be overpowering because the destructive force of fire can destroy any good luck coming into your living space. In the same way, water on the rooftop also constitutes a danger in feng shui, as it can symbolically drown you and wash away positive influences.

The shape of the Wood Element

Rectangular walls are good in the east and southeast.

The shape of the Earth Element

Square shapes are best in the dining room for harmony.

The shape of the Metal Element

Circles are suitable in the west and northwest.

The shape of the Water Element

Create the wave shape with blue for the Water Element in the north for career luck.

27 identifying and coping with inauspicious shapes

It is important to identify inauspicious shapes to improve the flow of chi in your home. These shapes may exist as part of the layout of your home, and be present in your furniture arrangement.

Some of the most commonly encountered inauspicious shapes reflected in floor plans are those which are made up of unbalanced combination of squares and rectangles, so that missing corners or incomplete shapes are created.

The examples shown here are S-shaped, N-shaped, and T-shaped arrangements. To remedy the imbalance, if you cannot alter the space of a room structurally due to lack of space or budget, or because you live in an apartment, then it is a good idea to keep that corner well lit in order to increase yang energy there. Otherwise, luck will be missing from this area.

Dealing with missing areas

Usually the best way of coping with missing areas is to use floor-length mirrors that have the effect of visually adding new space to the missing corner. But this remedy can only be used outside the bedrooms and kitchens. Another acceptable method is to enhance the energy of any missing areas by creating greater yang energy there, either with sounds, bright colors, or moving objects. This activates the chi that has become sluggish there, making it move and compensating for the unbalanced energy situated in those corners.

"S"-shaped layout

"N"-shaped layout

Keep the empty spaces well lit.

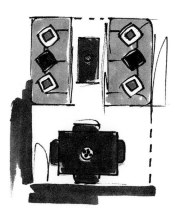

"T"-shaped layout

28 missing corners and what they mean

Missing corners are diagnosed according to which corner is missing in terms of its compass direction. Its effect depends on whether the missing corner represents your good or bad directions.

It indicates which member of the family's luck will be curtailed or affected. It also shows what kind of luck will be missing.

According to the Pa Kua method of feng shui, each of the eight compass corners of any home or any room is assigned one type of luck or life aspiration. To find out what type of luck is affected, therefore, it is necessary to first determine which compass direction the missing corner represents. Remember, as mentioned in Tip 7, use a good reliable compass to determine the orientation of your home's rooms, and then after you have superimposed the Lo Shu grid onto the floor plan, you will be able to see immediately which corner is missing. Then read on to see whose luck, and what kind of luck, is missing from the house. Also please note the remedies that are suggested for each corner.

The south sector

This affects the luck of respect, honor, recognition, and fame for those engaged in high-profile jobs or businesses. If this corner is missing, the good name of the family or its patriarch could get tarnished. To change and correct the luck here, add a mirror or some bright lights. The family member who will be affected by this luck is the middle daughter.

The southwest sector

This area affects the luck that is related to love, family, marriage, and romance. If this section is missing, it also causes the family's social life and popularity to suffer. The mother is seriously diminished, and the luck of the women of the household will also be reduced. To correct a missing southwest corner, place a cluster of natural quartz crystal here and shine a bright light on it.

The west sector

A missing corner in the west reduces the luck of the next generation. Your children will find it difficult to fulfill their ambitions – they will lack motivation and may feel alienated from the family. The most badly affected will be the young girls of the household, as the west area stands for the youngest daughter. Correct the imbalance of luck here by placing several six- or seven-rod metallic windchimes. The sounds of the windchimes will awaken the metal energy here, making it possible to redress the imbalance.

The northwest sector

In this area a missing corner will severely curtail the luck of the patriarch; sometimes, the husband

Curing missing corners

Missing northwest corner. Place six sets of six-rod windchimes here

Missing southwest corner. Place a crystal cluster here

This floor plan shows missing southwest and northwest corners, curtailing a family's popularity.

can be encouraged to leave the household. The family will also find it hard to attract helpful people or patrons, which is considered to be a severe affliction. The Chinese identify this luck as one of the most important kinds of luck for getting ahead and being successful. It is vital to either regularize this section with mirrors or build an extension here. If this is not possible, hang six sets of six-rod windchimes to make up for the missing corner.

The north sector

In this sector, a missing corner curtails the career prospects and success potential of the family members. Anyone with a missing north sector will find it hard to get a promotion at work or thrive afterwards. The best remedy is to place a water feature here with moving water, such as a small fountain or fish tank. This creates yang water which enhances the chi of this corner, and helps to correct the imbalance. A missing north sector particularly affects the fortunes of the middle son.

The northeast sector

A missing corner here affects the knowledge luck of the family. Literary pursuits will be hard to achieve, and those sitting examinations will find it harder to do well. A missing corner here is bad news for families with children who are still at school or who are attending college. The best way to correct a missing northeast corner is to place a large boulder there, or emphasize the Earth energy of this sector by painting the wall a prominent Earth color, such as yellow. A missing northeast corner affects the youngest son.

The east sector

In this area, a missing corner affects the family's good health, and the children of the family are especially affected. Correct this space by placing a strong and healthy plant in the east. A missing east sector is very bad also for descendants' luck, as it curtails the luck of the eldest son.

The southeast sector

This is a particularly bad area to be missing as it affects the wealth and income luck of the corner. When this part of the home is missing, the family wealth too suffers as it is affected in a negative way. Re-balance this area by painting the wall a bright green color or by placing a large plant here. Or better still, hang a wall mirror and let it reflect the plant thereby creating a garden effect in this particular corner.

If you use a yang water feature it will also do wonders for your wealth and your prosperity luck. A missing southeast corner reduces the luck of the eldest daughter.

29 using mirrors to cure missing corners

Mirrors are powerful expanders of energy and can be used in certain situations to deal with missing corners in the home. But be careful; if placed in the wrong area, they can create havoc.

In addition to using Element remedies in the home, as suggested previously, a more powerful way of dealing with missing corners is to fill in the corner with an extension or install a bright light to raise the energy of the missing area. Usually, some kind of overhead shelter is required for the remedy to take full effect. However, if you are on a budget or have space constraints, you may wish to use a full wall mirror to visually create space where it does not exist.

Placing wall mirrors

This solution, however, should only be used if the mirror does not have to be installed inside a bedroom. It is always important to remember that in solving one feng shui problem you do not want to create another bigger one. If you place a mirror wall inside a bedroom it brings in a great amount of unsettling energy, which can lead to some unfortunate consequences. So the main taboo for using mirrors to correct missing corners is not to put them on bedroom walls.

In the sketch shown on the right here, the missing corner of this apartment is occupied by the lift lobby. Here, it is easy enough to place a wall mirror on the wall of the living room as shown. If this missing corner is located in a compass direction where the luck of a family

When correcting a missing corner, such as the one shown here which is occupied by an elevator shaft, always use mirrors in living or dining areas rather than kitchens or bedrooms. You must make sure that any mirror you install does not reflect a toilet, a staircase, a bed, a door, or ugly scenery.

member is considered as particularly important to the residents' aspiration, this mirror cure should definitely be put into place. The mirror placed here will have the effect of visually expanding the space and correcting the missing corner.

30 guidelines for using wall mirrors

Wall mirrors can be excellent feng shui features, when placed correctly to expand an auspicious space or to visually extend into a missing corner as a remedy.

However, it is also important to remember the locations in which it is not advisable to place them at all.

Mirror placement

- Full wall mirrors should be high enough so that they do not seem to "cut" into the head of anyone, or cut off their feet, so it is best that they start from floor level.

- The wall mirror should ideally reflect an auspicious space, so it should not reflect a toilet, a staircase, a kitchen stove, or oven, and most importantly it should not directly reflect the main door, as this creates an immediate outflow of the fresh chi energy that has only just entered the home. If you have installed such a mirror, then place something between the mirror wall and the door so that you force the chi to linger and be diverted.

- It is best not to install mirrors anywhere in the bedroom, especially when it reflects the bed directly. This is a serious affliction and will create sleepless nights at best and severe problems between the couple sleeping on the bed at worst. If you have to have a mirror in the bedroom, never have it facing the bed, and cover it at night.

- Mirrors are excellent in the dining room as they symbolically double the food at the table. However, do not have

Mirror tiles should be large and not cause distortion. Healthy plants reflected in the mirror symbolically double the auspicious chi from the plant.

a mirror reflecting the kitchen stove, as this accentuates the Fire Element and has the effect of bringing about accidents for the residents.

- Mirrors are preferable to mirror tiles, but if you do use tiles, make sure that they do not cause any degree of distortion.

- Mirrors directly above a fireplace are a good feature as long as the mirror is not reflecting the door. In small spaces such as narrow foyer areas, hallways, or small corners, mirrors are excellent conductors of chi. Also, a mirror on the wall is excellent for breaking the monotony of a long narrow corridor, and for slowing chi.

31 protruding corners can strengthen luck

When home extensions are built, then the luck of the corner is extended, and the luck of the family member represented by that corner can be considerably enhanced.

However, extensions that stick out must be analyzed according to the Element attribute of the shape of the extension. You need to ensure that the shape of the extension does not represent an Element that clashes with the Element of the corner, or the overall shape of the home. This analysis can be undertaken by studying Element relationships according to the three Element cycles (see Chapter 3.)

Dining room extensions

In the example here, you can see that this apartment has a protruding corner in the dining room. This is auspicious since the dining room exerts an important effect on the family's fortunes. In this case, the corner represented is also the southeast, and the strengthening of this corner will enhance the wealth luck of the family. It will also benefit the eldest (or only) daughter of the family. As the extension here is not too large it will also not overwhelm the rest of the house – and the general shape of the home is rectangular, which signifies the Wood Element. Because the extension is in the southeast the Wood Element is further enhanced. Finally, the shape of the rectangular extension is also well balanced with the rest of the house, so overall this is an excellent example of a very lucky extension.

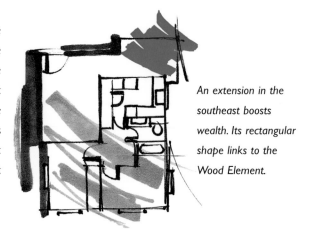

An extension in the southeast boosts wealth. Its rectangular shape links to the Wood Element.

Building in the west

If the extension is in the west, children's luck is enhanced, so it may help if you are having problems starting a family. The west also benefits the youngest daughter. However, a circular extension is best, as this relates to the shape of metal – the Element of the west.

If the extension you are planning is a rectangle, which you are adding to another rectangle, this is balanced and there will be no problems of Elements clashing as the extension and the main part of the house have the same shape.

When a semi-circular extension is added to a rectangle, you are adding Metal to Wood which is counter-productive as Metal destroys Wood. Also, adding a circular extension to a square house is not good as Metal exhausts Earth.

32 linking element shapes to your home

There are five basic shapes which link to the five elements, and these offer clues when you need to analyze the suitability of the shapes of objects, furniture, and structures within your living space.

Squares or rectangles

Square or rectangular shapes are generally the best to use, and these represent the Earth and Wood elements respectively. Furniture such as tables and cupboards are good when in these basic shapes as they signify support, security, and stability which are associated with the grounding energy of Earth and the growth energy of Wood. The square shape lends itself easily to feng shui enhancements based on compass guidelines, and is one of the best shapes to use in the home – it has no missing or protruding corner, is perfectly balanced, and resembles the Lo Shu Square. The Wood shape is usually an elongated rectangle and is considered very auspicious.

Circular shapes

Round or circular shapes belong to the Metal Element. Round structures and coffee tables send out strong energy that is associated with the Metal Element. It also signifies gold or money, which is why the Chinese are also so fond of round dining tables. The shape is also believed to represent heaven. Semi-circular extensions and bay windows are also thought to be auspicious, although as they are half circles there is the unfortunate connotation of being incomplete.

Circles link to the Metal Element, triangles show Fire, and wave shapes represent the Water Element.

Fire shapes

Pointed and triangular shapes with an apex link to Fire, so they signify rising yang energy. This shape is usually too strong for most people as the yang chi can be excessively dominating. So I usually do not recommend this shape for interiors.

Water shapes

These shapes are wavy. This is an Element that is best represented as subjects of decorative art pieces and in patterns and design motifs in interior decor, or shapes of curtains, for example, rather than being used as items of furniture or structures. However, give full rein to your creative skills, if you so desire. What is important is to make an energy field of the Element desired and this can be done in whatever way appeals to you.

33 shapes and their symbolic associations

According to many traditional feng shui masters, shapes can also be analyzed as friendly or hostile energy depending on what they look like and on what word, object, or animal they resemble.

Particular attention was paid in the old days to avoiding the use of shapes which resembled Chinese characters that had unlucky meanings. On a similar theme, they would often design buildings and floor plans in the shape of characters that had lucky meanings.

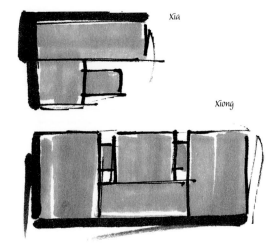

Xia

Xiong

The two shapes above are considered to be inauspicious since they resemble Chinese words that mean "Xia," or "down," and "Xiong," or bad luck, respectively. These two shapes are therefore considered very unlucky.

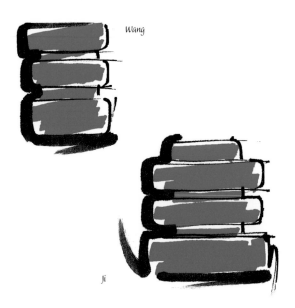

Wang

Ji

The shapes shown above resemble the Chinese characters "Ji," which means good luck, and "Wang," which means King. As both shapes are considered auspicious, designing a floor space or piece of furniture in these shapes would be deemed to bring good fortune to the user and the home.

Stepped or narrowing shapes

Shapes that look like steps, or which resemble a narrowing at the mid-point, are regarded as inauspicious, as the connotations are thought to be negative. The Chinese have always been suspicious of anything irregular or asymmetrical since imbalance of this sort is anathema to good luck. If you are not sure about a shape, it is always best to opt for ones that look complete and balanced, with all the sides of a similar height and width.

34 auspicious shapes for tables

One of the best dining table shapes to use in the home is round, although rectangular, square, or the eight-sided Pa Kua shape can also enhance your luck.

Always select the dining table with care, as the feng shui implications are significant.

Round dining tables

These are always preferred by the Chinese, because in addition to representing the auspicious gold element, a circular shape also denotes that everything to do with the family's wealth and continued wellbeing will proceed smoothly. Parents and children are considered to have a greater chance of maintaining harmonious relationships when the dining table is round. Usually, however, the round dining table needs to seat at least eight people and upwards with three generations seated eating together. This means the family's wealth luck will continue through the generations.

Square and rectangular dining tables

A dining table that is square signifies the stability of the Earth Element, but these should not seat more than four people. If you have eight people seated at a square table it is considered less auspicious.

Rectangular tables should never be too long as this can suggest members of the family losing touch with each other. While long tables will not

A round dining table is always auspicious; a square table attracts the stability of the Earth Element.

impede the growth of family wealth, they do little to help family togetherness. It is for this reason that the Chinese almost always never have a long rectangular table in their residential dining rooms.

Pa Kua dining tables

The Pa Kua, or eight-sided dining table, is ideal for marking out the eight different directions, with each side being especially suited to a different member of the family. My own family dining table is a Pa Kua shape which symbolizes all of the Five Elements, making it very auspicious. However, I do place a lazy Susan in the center of my dining table. This has been specially designed in glass (to signify the stable Earth energy) on which has been etched the very auspicious symbol of the double fish.

When the dining table is an auspicious design with maximum yang energy, and is constantly seen heaped high with food, the family fortunes should stay intact and expand with the passing years.

35 lucky shapes for decorative objects

Vases and bowls filled with water and flowers in the home always represent good feng shui. As well as generating yang energy, such decorative objects represent the best of the Five Elements.

Let me explain. In feng shui all of the Universe can be reduced to one of Five Elements – Earth, Water, Fire, Metal, and Wood – and all of these Elements always have either a yang or a yin side. For homes to enjoy good fortune and bring residents continued success in the pursuit of happiness and prosperity, the yang side of all Five Elements should be present inside homes.

Element imbalances

If the chi of any home degenerates to the extent that there is element imbalance caused by the shortage or excess of one element, then illness and bad luck will occur. On the other hand, when elements such as Water, Earth, and Wood are present and these are more yang than yin, then the feng shui of the space is instantly enhanced and activated, causing the chi to flow smoothly around.

Vases and water-filled bowls with flowers create good yang energy.

Vases of flowers

Vases and bowls filled with water and flowers create this yang energy very efficiently. But it is always better to choose vases and bowls that have auspicious shapes as this will add even more to the enhancement of chi inside the home. Vases are best when there is some sort of a neck, with a fatter round base as this shape suggests that the vase can retain its good chi. Vases in the home should never be left standing upright when empty. They should either be put away, or displayed containing some water. When the vase is left standing empty it can cause a loss of income, leading to reduced circumstances for the household.

Empty bowls standing ready

Bowls should also be fat looking and have a definite rim. Bowls are regarded differently from vases because their shape is naturally auspicious. They may be left empty and, indeed, many Chinese homes are decorated with large, empty bowls. This signifies the bowl is ready to receive good chi coming into the home.

Bowls that are ceramic, crystal, or another earth-based material such as porcelain or china are especially auspicious as they are believed to bring in good grounding Earth energy.

36

avoid split levels in the home

Split-level homes can cause problems for the people living in them, particularly the patriarch. The unstable energy that exists can cause different types of bad luck and misfortune.

Generally, split and multiple floor levels within the home are not encouraged by experienced feng shui practitioners. This is because multi-levels cause serious disruptions in the flow of chi and affect the smooth entry of good fortune into the home. Also, the different floor levels also cause energy to become unstable. To have one floor as the main living area is preferred, and indeed homes whose interiors have been designed to have multiple levels are said to be most inauspicious. And I have to confess that I myself have seen some multi-level homes suffer from the most unexpected and horrendous misfortunes.

Houses with split levels

One prominent family had their world crash in on them after they moved into a new home that was built with five split levels. The multiple levels of floor had created an environment of instability within the home which ended in serious problems for the head of the house. This was because in their case the main door had been located in the northwest sector and it was placed on the lowest of the five levels. Shortly after they had moved into their new mansion, the father was charged with embezzlement.

Another family saw the patriarch struck down by a particularly severe stroke that left him

A lush growing plant placed at the lower of the two levels suggests growth and upward mobility and will equalize the energy levels.

partially paralyzed soon after they had moved into their new home. The house had again been designed with multiple levels. In this case the many different levels had been made much worse by the fact that the ceilings of this house had large exposed hostile beams that seemed to press threateningly down on residents when they were sitting below. Probably these two very inauspicious features conspired to create havoc with the family's health and longevity luck.

37 useful remedies for split-level homes

If you are living in a split-level home and you can't move, you need to create some grounding energy to stabilize the unsettling environment that exists.

If you are occupying a home with split levels and cannot do anything to change the situation, and if there are two or more different floor levels, then the best remedy for the situation is to bring plenty of large decorative plants into the home. This enhances the power of the Wood chi, and because Wood energy controls Earth energy, this ensures that there will be a much more stable, grounding environment created inside the home.

Also, the decorative plants will symbolically send roots into the ground and create further stability for the home's feng shui. This remedy is the best way of overcoming the unstable grounding energy caused by the split levels.

In addition, always remember that the lowest of the floor levels should be the room used as the living room, while the higher level should be used as the dining area.

Placing healthy plants on the lower level enhances the Earth Element in a split-level home, giving it stability. Always eat on the upper level and have the living room on the lowest level.

38 chi should meander

The essence of good feng shui is always to do with positive energy flow. Auspicious energy always flows slowly and meanders, while sharp, unlucky energy always moves fast and in a straight line.

This lucky and unlucky characteristic of the flow of chi applies equally in the larger environment as well as in the smaller environment of the living space. For you to enjoy good feng shui it is imperative that you arrange your furniture, and position your entrances, in such a way that the chi that enters your space comes in slowly but positively. The chi must always be allowed to slow down, meander, revolve, and accumulate.

Chi needs to flow freely around the home, unobstructed by clutter which causes chi to stagnate.

Healthy chi

Chi entering a home must never do so in a rush. This can occur when it comes up a long straight driveway towards a house's entrance, or when it comes along a long straight corridor in front of your apartment door (see Tip 51.)

Care should be taken to ensure that chi always stays vibrant, that it must never be allowed to stagnate. This happens when rooms are left empty and unoccupied over long periods of time, when there is clutter, or when windows never get opened so that musty smells prevail. Rooms that are never cleaned also tend to create stale energy.

Chi flow

Once you understand how chi moves and circulates, you will be able to apply the principles of chi flow to your home layout and arrangement of furniture. Always have a focal piece of furniture in each room and try to place it in such a way that the chi entering the room is encouraged to move round the furniture. Chi first enters the home through the main door and flows out through secondary doors, windows and the back door. Inside the living room, chi moves gently through the open space and stops when there are pieces of furniture or decorative items or plants. The more chi is allowed to curve and turn the better it will be. Important doors inside the home should not face each other as this creates a straight, rather than a curving flow of energy. Good chi fills rooms with vibrant energy. So let chi circulate gently before it moves on. Auspicious chi is always subtle and slow and fills the air with crisp, clean energy.

39 position your doors skillfully

All the doors of your home have a significant effect on its feng shui, with the most important door being the main, front, door.

The main door is usually defined as the door that is the most frequently used by residents to get in and out of the house. Usually, the main door should not be difficult to identify. Sometimes, however, there can be two or more doors that can qualify as the main door under other definitions (see also Tip 10.) These other definitions for main door are:

- The door facing the general orientation of the home itself.

- The door facing the direction that has maximum yang energy (such as the main road.)

- The door that is the largest door in the home.

Finding the main door

When there is doubt as to which is the main door of the home, feng shui masters usually take the door that follows the general orientation of the home. But if you have several options, then it is advisable to make it clear that you designate the door you are most comfortable with as your main door. If this is also a door that faces one of your auspicious directions, then it will certainly bring you some good feng shui. When you and all the occupants of your home consider the door as the main door, you will help to focus your personal chi on it.

When there are two doors to a room it is better that they are diagonal to each other rather than confronting each other. This will then cause the chi to meander, thereby accumulating auspicious energy.

Positioning doors well

In any case, pay some attention to all the doors of your home, from the front door to the back door, as well as all the in-between doors and the doors into each of the main rooms. Make sure they are all positioned skillfully so that they are not directly facing each other. Here are a few helpful guidelines that you can use as a checklist:

- Doors should be of the same size, but the main door should ideally be slightly larger.

- Doors are best when they are placed diagonally opposite each other.

40 have a solid door facing a "bright hall"

The main door to your home should be solid and made from wood. This is because the front entrance is where chi first enters, and it is considered the "mouth" of the home.

For a door to be considered auspicious, especially the main door, it should be solid. This means that a door made of solid wood is always better than one made of glass. In the old days, all the main doors into Chinese family mansions would not only be made of solid wood they would also look big, strong, and imposing. This is because the main door is said to be the "mouth" of the home and it is the symbol of entry. It therefore needs to be strong and secure for protection.

Two doors directly facing each other are said to be confrontational. It also causes chi to move in a straight line and this creates "killing energy." The most ideal situation is when a main door opens into an open space both inside as well as outside the home. Placing a bright light just above the foyer in front of the door is another excellent feng shui enhancer.

Opening onto a "bright hall"

Ideally, it should open inwards into a "bright hall," and open outwards also to a bright hall. This is a patch of space that can be a foyer inside the home and a garden outside. The bright hall effect allows chi to settle, gather, and accumulate before and after it enters the home. The slowing down effect of chi transforms anything that may have been afflicted or hostile into something more friendly and inviting. In my own home, I have created bright halls that are as big as rooms both inside and outside the main door. In addition, I have also placed a pair of Fu dogs outside and red carpet between the dogs. This ensures that the chi has no problem identifying which is my main door.

However, because I also have a second main door (this is to accommodate the fact that my husband and I have different auspicious directions,) I do the same thing for the second door as well, although in this second main door the bright hall effect is much smaller.

Harmful feng shui

An important bonus in having two "main" doors like this is that it enables me to close one door during the years when it is afflicted by harmful annual flying stars (see last chapter.) This is a very important bonus as it is a feature that enables us to escape the bad effect of the hostile and sickness stars by giving us an alternative door to use. Remember that the chi that affects your feng shui is not static. It is dynamic and constantly changing and being influenced by both tangible and intangible energy. Understanding the nature,

flow, and whereabouts of this energy, both good and bad, is what feng shui practice is about. A lot of the time common sense will help in understanding this energy. But when you also know the different methods of using feng shui formulas, your understanding of energy will be much more enhanced. So always use your understanding to protect the feng shui of your main door. No matter which formula you use, if your main door enjoys good chi and good energy everyone in the home will benefit from it.

Always remember:

- Doors should always open inwards and never outwards. Luck should flow in and not out, unless it is the back door – this is the only exception.

- Avoid "eye-to-eye" doors. This refers to door knobs that directly face each other that cause residents to be confrontational, rather than accommodating of each other. Replace these knobs with long handles.

Long door handles like the one illustrated above are a good solution to "eye-to-eye" doorknobs. The circular base is auspicious, and the flowing shape of the handle avoids creating poison arrows that may be caused by a more angular design.

41 neutralize blocks to success

If you have structures outside your home that form a "block" or an "obstacle" to the chi entering, they can restrict your success and will need to be screened or dissipated.

Blocks to success happen when there are structures that signify "obstacles" that seem threatening or harmful to the main door. Examples of blocks to success and harmony are pillars, elevators that open directly into your main door, trees, edges of buildings, and telegraph poles. These blocks to success should be neutralized by hanging the powerful eight-sided Pa Kua mirror (see Tip 14.)

The Pa Kua mirror, however, needs to be used with caution. It only works if it can be hung high on the outside above the main door and facing outwards. If you do this, always position the mirror so that it faces the obstacle that you need to deflect, rather than facing the front door, for example, of friendly neighbors. Please note, as mentioned before, the Pa Kua should never be hung inside the house as it can do more harm than good.

Obstacles to success that hit the main door can also be blocked from view. You can do this with thick curtains, a wall, a divider of some kind, and even some foliage plants, small trees, or a hedge. Whatever method you choose to use depends on your own circumstances and where your house or apartment is situated. The key is to block or to dissolve the harmful energy that emanates towards your home from the obstacle.

When the main door opens directly to face a single tree or a solid wall, the symbolism of obstruction is felt on a daily basis. It is a good idea to decorate the area so as to visually camouflage the obstructions.

42 overcoming the ferocious tiger and injured dragon

There are various remedies you can call upon when your main door is confronted by these two particular feng shui afflictions.

You need to check to see if either or both of the following type of afflictions affects your home. Different problems can confront houses and apartments.

Facing the tiger's mouth

For houses, this means facing the entrance to a subway station, or facing a long tunnel, or if you live out in the country, facing a cave or a cave-like entrance of some kind. For apartments, this means your door directly facing a down escalator or an elevator shaft, or a rubbish chute. These examples are said to be the tiger's mouth because the chi in front of your home is perpetually being drawn downwards, therefore slowly but surely siphoning your wealth away and causing your health to suffer as well. Overcome the ferocity of the tiger by placing powerful lions on both sides of your door on the outside. These are the Fu dogs that are said to possess the mysterious ability to confront and overcome the hostile tiger.

Facing the stagnating dragon

This situation occurs when your main door faces a dustbin or chute, or stagnating rubbish. Make an effort to have the area in front of your home cleaned up. It is really worth spending the money.

Avoid placing dustbins close to the front door. Here, it is best to swap with the plant, and remedy the presence of the dustbin with a windchime by the front door.

Another equally bad situation is when your door is directly facing anything that has a grid pattern or design. This can be caused by lights placed in a net pattern of grid lines or any kind of fencing around your building that resembles prison walls. This is said to be the stagnating or injured dragon and the chi that comes into your home is flawed, causing you to suffer from bad luck. With this type of luck, you cannot make any kind of progress in your life and illness will be a common occurrence in your home. Usually, when you suspect the presence of an injured dragon, then placing the image (which can be a painting or a sculpture) of a healthy dragon outside your home will overcome this situation. Do not worry about making the dragon image too big.

43

what to do when faced with a sleeping dragon

It is never good for your home to face a parking lot or an abandoned house as musty, stagnant chi will blow towards your front door. You need to use cures to confront this afflicted energy.

When the main door of the apartment block you live in, or of your home, is in front of a parking lot, the symbolism is inauspicious as this means things coming to a stop directly in front of you. The meaning of stagnation is very strong, and this can tend to impede your progress through life. To overcome this, it is a good idea to hang rather large tinkling windchimes on both sides of your main door. However, do not hang the windchimes on the door – and never walk under a windchime. This means not hanging chimes directly above your front door. The sounds of the chime will counter everything coming to a standstill.

Sleeping dragons

When you face an abandoned, dilapidated house or an empty building you should know that energy that is blowing towards your home from that direction is seriously flawed. Old historical buildings that have been left empty are the worst, since chi inside such buildings is stale, musty, old, and unhappy. When you face such a sight, it could bring you ruin or some serious misfortune. Paint your door a bright glistening white and use lots of lights that are full of powerful and alive yang energy. You can also place strong growing plants outside your door to overcome the smell of stagnation coming from the building. Sleeping dragons, such as these buildings, can be dangerous. If you are facing a demolished site where new construction is taking place, the chi is no longer harmful. However, while construction is going on the energy is unbalanced and disturbed. Protect yourself from this feng shui affliction by placing some kind of divider – planting some trees, closing the curtains or using some lights should do the trick.

44 remedies for doors in a straight line

All the doors of the home are natural conduits of energy. However, when two or three doors are aligned in a straight line, the chi turns malevolent.

This positioning of doors in a straight line is one of the most harmful of feng shui taboos and quite a common problem in apartments. Most internal doors are kept open, and over the years, as furniture and possessions build up the doors that are in a straight line with each other become so much a part of the household they tend to get ignored. If the front and back door are aligned in a straight line any luck entering the home instantly flies right out through the back door again. This is therefore a very inauspicious situation.

Doors facing each other

When doors directly face each other, they tend to be confrontational, leading to quarrels and hostile energy. Hanging a painting, placing a small decorative sideboard, or even a plant next to the doors will serve to distract the chi, thereby representing some kind of cure. It is better not to use mirrors to reflect doors.

Alternatively, place a divider as a distraction so that chi is encouraged to flow around the divider. Or hang a painting or a windchime to soften the effect and create balance.

Another manifestation of afflicted doors that might skip the awareness of residents, is a sliding door to a balcony that is placed directly opposite the entrance door. This is usually found in high-

rise blocks or condominiums. Here, too, chi entering will get dissipated almost as soon as it comes into the home.

Shown here are three doors in a straight line. To overcome this, use clever furnishings such as screens or heavy drapes, or better still place low cabinets or tables in front of the center door. This forces the chi to make a turn.

45 using a horse for protection

There may be other structures facing your home that can cause problems but these can be resolved. Using a statue of a standing horse by the front door can give you protection.

Not all structures in front of your main door cause big problems, so do guard against getting paranoid about any obstacles there may be. Many of these features simply cause stumbling blocks and hiccups in your life, they are irritating and inconvenient, but they are easily corrected and should not cause you to become upset. But if by now you are beginning to feel overwhelmed by the effect of structures around your living space, don't be; being interested in feng shui involves developing a keen eye and an awareness of your environment. It will help you to develop a sensitivity to the energies that surround your living and work spaces.

What's opposing you?

The following list pinpoints a few small structures and features that may be facing your front door, either indoors or outdoors, that could cause you to stumble – deal with them and they should not hurt you.

When you place a single horse inside the foyer of your home, it creates wonderful yang energy. Rearing horses, however, can be overpowering, so follow your instincts when choosing a horse to ensure it does not create imbalance.

Inauspicious features

Check out the afflictions listed below:

- Facing problem shapes, for example the tombstone shape brings illness, while the fire shape can encourage quarrels.

- Being opposite water hydrants or "for sale" signs from across the road.

- Facing crosses, either upright or diagonal crosses.

- Being opposed by a dead tree stump.

- Facing poles, pillars, and other vertical structures.

- Being opposite children's playgrounds as the slides and swings here can be a source of some problems. This is because they resemble poison arrows, again causing cutting chi to affect your home. Also, because slides and swings are often in constant use, their negative impact is magnified.

A horse for protection

To overcome these small obstacles is simple enough. The remedy requires us to take a leaf out of the martial arts stance "to sit like a horse." This means literally to stand so firm that nothing makes you stumble. The synonym of the horse is well known among martial art enthusiasts. They know how to "chor mah" – which means standing so firm that nothing can shake you. Learn to anchor your home firmly and nothing can shake your good fortune. One way of doing this is simply to place the image of a strong, standing horse – reproductions of the Tang Horse are ideal – near your front door. The image of the horse is regarded as a symbol of good fortune. In addition to bringing your family honor and recognition, it also signifies a firm foundation.

46

watch out for thunder striking from heaven

Your home can get serious afflictions due to some of the configurations of apartment or office buildings in city environments, particularly if you live close by.

There is a serious problem that can harm people whose buildings face either the south or the northwest directions. If this is the direction faced by your apartment block, then go out and investigate if there are two tall buildings facing it. It is bad enough when you are facing a tall building since this is like confronting a mountain, but when you face two buildings, and there is a narrow gap or road between the two buildings and the gap is directly facing your apartment entrance, then it is described in the books that thunder and lightning chi from the heavens will travel though the gap, turning into killing chi and hit your building.

A building facing the south or northwest

You only need to be afraid of this configuration when it is in the direction of northwest or south from your building. It is more harmful if it lies to the south of your building and is facing your entrance. To protect yourself, it is important to "earth" your home. So, near the entrance to the door of your apartment, on both the outside and the inside, place a patch of strong Earth Element, for example a faux marble, marble, or granite floor. This will "earth" your home to protect it from the lightning killing chi from the heavens!

Chi rushing between two high-rise buildings in the northwest or south symbolize heaven and fire, or thunder in the sky.

The above cure is also excellent for buildings and houses that face powerful transmitters, railway tracks, or whose homes are in the flight path of airplanes. These are serious health hazards.

Even when you do not have these features threatening you, it is a good idea to place a patch of stone material (about 3ft [920cm] square) in front of your door. This can be concrete, marble, terrazzo, slate, or even plain cement – it is a most powerful protection. If you have a front entrance hall made of stone this gives you a built-in feng shui protective system. But if you have carpets or wood flooring, consider investing in a stone foyer area.

47

identify your corners of good fortune

Good fortune corners inside the home are usually the corners that are diagonally across from the main door into the room. So you will have a good fortune corner for the house, and one in every room.

If this corner is missing, your luck gets curtailed and you should definitely install a mirror to visually restore this area. If this corner is protruding, the luck is said to be doubled if you succeed in activating the chi here correctly.

Finding your lucky corners

So always identify the lucky corners of your home, and then plan to activate the chi in each corner so that everyone benefits. Look at the following list to see how you can protect, as well as energize, your lucky corners. In the bedrooms, you should be a little more careful and observe the usual taboos of the bedroom (see Tips 53–67.) Otherwise, have fun activating your lucky corners. Firstly, make sure that your lucky corner does not have a toilet or a store room on the other side of the

The corner that is diagonal to the door is the lucky corner.

wall. If there is a toilet near the wall on the other side, place a metal object here so that this energy will help prevent the afflicted energy seeping through.

Activating your corners

Activate the lucky corner by enhancing its chi:

- If the corner is in the south of your living room, place a plant here to simulate Wood, which feeds the Fire chi of the corner.

- If the corner is southwest or northeast, place bright lights to simulate Fire which feeds the Earth energy that is present here.

- For a west or northwest corner, place a cluster of natural crystals or a marble statue here to create Earth chi which will add to the gold or metal of the corner.

- If the direction of the lucky spot of the living room is north, place strong Metal energy there to boost Water – the element of the north.

- For an eastern or southeastern corner, place a water feature in the form of an aquarium or a small table fountain, as the Water Element enhances Wood.

48

curved staircases are the best

Staircases are important conduits of chi in any home, and some care should be taken to make them auspicious.

When the staircase is not auspicious, the main effect is that money and upward advancement are hard to come by. So if you live in a house or an apartment that has two main levels, take a good look at your staircase. The common staircases of apartment buildings used by all tenants are deemed to be outside your living space. However, common stairs should also have as many good feng shui features as possible.

To start with, make your staircase safe, solid, wide, and not too steep. Precarious looking staircases with gaps or holes are very inauspicious.

Curved staircases

Curved staircases are believed to be the best, as they slow down the passage of chi and force it to meander its way through the home. Spiral staircases are not as auspicious and should be confined to the outdoors as garden staircases. Spiral staircases can be harmful when they are inside the house and placed in the center of the home. Here it is believed that they resemble corkscrews that hurt the heart of the home. When your staircase curves around, but is solid and has proper banisters, it is deemed to be as good as a completely curved staircase. Straight staircases are fine, they do no harm, but you may need to slow the chi down if they are opposite the front door.

Staircases are best when placed by the side of the home and preferably the dragon side, that is on the east, or it can also be the left side of the home (looking out.) Do not be confused by this statement. The dragon side has two definitions because sometimes it is defined in terms of compass direction. But to be on the safe side, use the left side to denote the dragon side inside the home. Placing the staircase on the dragon side brings upward mobility in career and business.

Staircases should ideally be broader at the bottom than at the top as this signifies loads of wealth entering the inner confines of the home.

Also, make sure the staircase does not start from the main door as the chi will move up the stairs too quickly. If it does, use some form of divider.

Curved staircases attract excellent chi to your home.

49

be careful what you put under the staircase

It is very important to be aware of the items you put under your staircase. To start with, never place something under it that you would never want to step upon.

A good friend of mine was dumb enough to set up his son's computer and study table under the large staircase of their home. Visually, it looked very good but in the three months the poor boy spent there doing his homework his grades suffered so dramatically that the whole family are now firm believers in feng shui. Naturally, when the desk was removed from under the staircase, his grades returned to normal.

Taboos for under the stairs

So never place anyone's table or work desk there. Worse still, never, never place an altar under the staircase. Apart from this being very disrespectful, it really does create very bad karma, which in turn

A storeroom under the staircase is fine, but do not place prayer books or important files inside. They get stepped on day after day!

will cause obstacles in your life. I have always told people who want to place altars inside their homes that they must learn how to do this correctly, and also to watch the feng shui of their placement. Otherwise, altars will simply do more harm than good. And please do not think that altars are purely spiritual places that have nothing to do with your feng shui. Both spiritual practices and feng shui are to do with energy. Note the following guidelines on other things to avoid.

Loss of wealth

Do not place a bar under the stairs. This is another common usage of the space under a big staircase. If the bar is next to the staircase it is fine, but if it is under it and includes a tap there, this will symbolize the family losing their wealth – everything just drains away. And if you are unlucky enough to have gold faucets, this really means your wealth and all you gold being drained away – so do be careful.

Finally, never place an indoor water feature or pond under the staircase. This causes harm to the next generation of the household and can adversely influence their luck.

Storerooms situated under the staircase are fine. Keeping the storerooms filled with family paraphernalia is good feng shui.

50 what's at the top of your staircase?

The top of your staircase should ideally face a wall that is decorated with inspiring or auspicious pictures. However, never use offputting pictures or depict frightening wild animals.

So let's investigate exactly what is facing your staircase as you look up at it. At the top, try not to let the staircase face a door that leads into a toilet. It is better for it to face a bedroom, but best of all is for the staircase to meet a wall that is decorated with some pleasant or auspicious painting. The wall should be at least 3ft (920cm) from the top of the staircase. In my home the staircase faces a wall on which I hang a very large thangka – a Tibetan religious painting of the Medicine Buddha. For me, personally, there is nothing more auspicious than this but you need to choose what inspires you.

An inspiring piece of art

Always hang something there that means good things to you. This can be a painting of pleasant scenery, oriental art, a sailing ship – anything that makes you happy and inspired.

Do not hang paintings of fierce or wild animals as this creates a frightening influence.

Hanging paintings of mountains is not a good idea as they can cause your chi to get blocked.

Paintings with sharp corners, triangles, and other hostile patterns will also not be good or ultimately inspiring for you.

You are probably beginning to understand the philosophy now, so use the same guidelines when you select any wallpaper designs.

The first thing you see upon climbing your staircase each day after work should be an inspiring or auspicious image.

When the staircase faces a door it is quite bad, but facing a door that opens into the toilet is worse. If the staircase faces a balcony upstairs, it can cause a loss of wealth, so it is better to close this up. It has the same effect if it faces a window. If closing off the staircase is not practical, screen off doors, windows, or balconies or hang heavy drapes.

51 corridors are important purveyors of chi

Corridors strongly affect the flow of chi through the home. Long corridors should be decorated to distract the chi, forcing it to slow down and accumulate.

But long corridors are also conduits of energy, so decorate them in an attractive way. Because long and straight corridors cause chi to become harmful, feng shui masters always advise against placing rooms right at the end of long corridors. But long corridors are not really difficult to correct. The idea is to distract the flow of chi, so that you slow it down. This can be done by placing something to block the visual view of a long corridor – this can be a potted plant, a painting, a windchime, hollow bamboo stems tied with red thread, or a small cabinet.

If your room is placed right at the end of a long corridor, the effect is like being at the end of a T junction, where the killing breath rushes headlong at you. So do remember, it is important to slow down the flow of chi.

A broad corridor filled with attractive items causes chi to slow down.

Bad lighting in corridors

The biggest problem about long and narrow corridors is that if they are badly lit, they trap yin energy, or cause the existing chi to become stale. There cannot be anything more inauspicious – I usually recommend that, if possible, corridors are made to curve and that they are well lit.

When choosing lighting for corridors, it should be designed to stimulate the best feng shui energies. There should not be any dingy corners where beneficial energy can stagnate and grow stale and vapid. This is what causes bad feng shui, and it can manifest itself in illness, listlessness, and tiredness. Wherever possible, natural light should be allowed to come into corridors. So don't close off windows near corridors with blinds or curtains. Where artificial light supplements natural light, it should be gentle and indirect.

When there are rooms that open off corridors in a home, it is better that the doors do not face each other in a confrontational mode as this suggests a certain amount of conflict arising between residents of the rooms. Placing crystals on a low table near the sides of these doors will reduce the build up of hostility chi as they bring good energy, particularly to well-lit places.

This bed directly faces a large mirror. This is probably one of the worst examples of a mirror inside the bedroom, causing the relationship between the sleeping couple to deteriorate with serious consequences. It is a good idea to remove the mirror. The fan directly above the bed is not a good feature but it is better above the feet than directly above the head. Lamps directly above the sleeping couple's head are not a good feature, so it's best to remove them and place the lights by the side of the bed instead. The painting next to the bed is excellent if it is suitable for a bedroom; unsuitable subjects are wild animals, water, a lake or a water scene, a dragon, or any kind of deity. It is not a good idea to hang a picture of Christ or Buddha in your bedroom unless you are single, in which case place the painting directly behind you, and never in front of you with your feet directly facing it.

55 examine the effects of toilets on your bed

There are several ways the toilet can cause bad feng shui when you're sleeping, and these need to be firmly dealt with so that you can benefit from good feng shui energy in the bedroom.

There are several different ways that toilets can be harmful in the bedroom in relation to the positioning of the bed.

When the bed is placed against a wall and the toilet is on the other side, this means that the bed is sharing a wall with the toilet, which is always draining energy, and the chi entering the sleeping person is very seriously afflicted. This is not a good position, and the bed should be placed against another wall. If you really cannot move the bed away from this particularly harmful position, then use red wallpaper or paint that wall red to symbolically burn the bad energy that is seeping through. The only problem is that red walls are not the ideal color for the bedroom. Nevertheless, this is considerably less harmful than being afflicted by the toilet.

The bad energy, however, is reduced when the toilet is placed against another wall inside the bathroom. If you just move the bed a little way away from the wall, this should be enough to overcome the effects of the bad chi. Otherwise, it is always better to move the bed against another wall. Remember that even if this happens to be the best direction according to the Kua formula (see Chapter 4) you should not use this direction.

A toilet door facing the bed

If your bed is positioned so that the door into the toilet is directly facing the head of the bed, this is an equally bad situation. If you can manage it, do re-arrange the position of the bed. If you can't move it, always keep the door to the toilet closed or re-hang the door. If there is room inside the bathroom, it is worth placing some kind of a plastic curtain to block out the view of the toilet.

A toilet on the floor above

Make sure that there is no toilet on the floor directly above your bed. This is one of the most vexing things about apartment living. If yours is a block where every floor is similar, then this danger is considerably lessened, but if the design layouts vary, then do find out where the toilets of the upper floor are located. You can then re-arrange your bed to avoid bad influence from the toilets above.

Toilets opposite, above or sharing a wall with a bed cause bad energy.

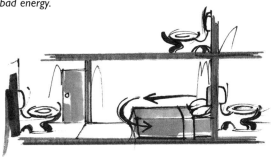

56 watch the grain of wooden floorboards

Another thing that you should watch out for in the bedroom is that there is nothing there that cuts across your sleeping chi.

Probably the most obvious affliction that applies to this guideline is when the wooden floorboards of your bedroom run counter to the bedroom placement. For example, if you have a rectangular bedroom the boards should span the length of the room, rather than having more boards running across the room's width. Equally, the wood grain of each board should run straight and the grain of adjoining boards should not appear to cut into each other.

For the same reason, wooden floors with a criss-cross or herringbone design are not good feng shui in the bedroom because this represents energy in conflict.

If your bedroom suffers from any of these afflictions, the chi of the bedroom is said not to be harmonious with your sleeping position. The best way to overcome this situation is simply to place a solid, single-color carpet under the bed so that the bed itself is standing on the carpet and not on the floorboards.

Do make sure that the bed boards on a bed's base are aligned in accordance with the sleeper. Those that are not could be sending out imbalanced energy to the sleeping form, which can eventually show itself in aches and pains in the body. If you have this problem, use a thick or thicker mattress or change your bed.

Double mattresses are best

Couples who sleep in double beds should use one double size mattress rather than two single size mattresses. Even if these are joined by a zip, it still indicates that there will be division at some point in the relationship.

57

beds at an angle pose a tough problem

One of the most vexing dilemmas in practicing bedroom feng shui happens when you try to tap into your best direction based on the Eight Mansions or Kua formula (see Chapter 4.)

This states that every person is born with four auspicious and four inauspicious directions relating to the compass. One of the most important applications of this formula on directions is your best sleeping direction. While in theory it is easy enough to find your auspicious directions, in practice few rooms are oriented in such a way that you can actually have your bed facing exactly the direction you want. Usually the reality is that to get the directions accurate, you will need to place your bed at an angle to the wall.

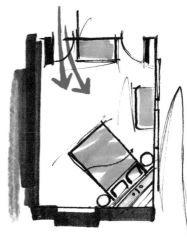

When you place the bed at an angle in order to tap your best direction, be certain that the triangular area behind the bed is filled up and not left empty.

Place your bed in a good direction

So to tap into your good directions or to avoid your bad directions, you may well have to place your bed in such a way that it is at an angle to the wall. This means aligning your sleeping direction to allow your head to receive good fortune and success chi from your best direction. This could mean that you end up sleeping on a bed that does not have the solid support of a wall, which then means you will be lacking in support!

My feeling on this issue is that I would rather sleep with a full and solid wall behind me. One feng shui master disagrees with this, and he is the master who is probably the world's most ardent exponent of Eight Mansions feng shui. You the reader will have to decide on this particular issue.

I feel very disoriented and strange when I sleep at an angle to the walls of my room. I feel this is seriously lacking in balance and symmetry, two principles that are the cornerstones of good feng shui practice. As such I am prepared to sacrifice using the Eight Mansions formula if I have to choose.

Happily, in my own home this is not an issue since from the start I oriented my home in such a way that all the rooms of my house have walls that are easy to apply the principles of formula feng shui to. If you live in rented premises or apartments, however, you have to make your own decision. If you want to tap into your best direction, and don't want a triangular empty space behind you because your bed is at an angle, place built-in cupboards behind. This is an effective compromise.

58 take note of sleeping taboos in the bedroom

There are several feng shui taboos on how you place your bed and arrange your bedroom furniture to prevent bad chi.

When you are sleeping, you are vulnerable to absorbing bad-luck chi into your system that manifests itself in misfortunes, accidents, or loss. So to ensure against this, it is a good idea to know about some basic taboos that have to do with protecting against bad chi in your bedroom during your sleeping hours.

Beds on the floor

Try not to sleep on the floor as this can result in excessive absorption of yin energy. It is not so bad if your home is in a high-rise apartment, and there is wood or carpet on the floor of your bedroom, but those who live in basement or ground-level

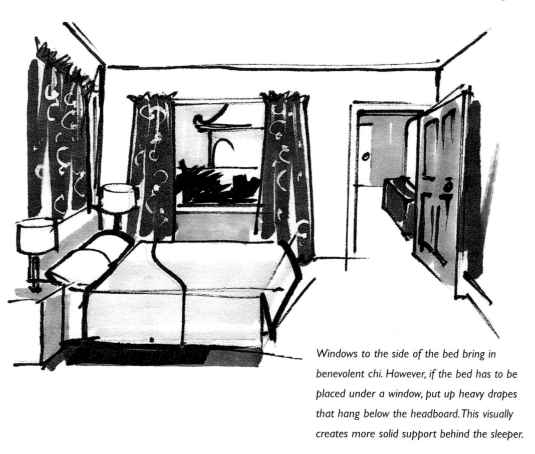

Windows to the side of the bed bring in benevolent chi. However, if the bed has to be placed under a window, put up heavy drapes that hang below the headboard. This visually creates more solid support behind the sleeper.

bedrooms should refrain from sleeping on the floor. Sleeping on the floor is also even more unfortunate if your feet are directly pointing at the door as this is considered an inauspicious position. Your luck becomes badly afflicted and your health will be negatively affected.

Never sleep on a bed that is too small for you. This seriously constricts your career and business progress. It also symbolizes failure to grow. Those who sleep on beds that are too short for them are particularly affected. Growing children will also have their progress blocked, so do take note of this feng shui problem and change your children's beds as they grow. It is always better for the bed to be too large than too small.

Sleeping on top bunks

It is also not a good idea to sleep on beds that are too high as this will always make you prone to accidents. The best way to guard against this is to make certain that should you fall off the bed you do not get hurt. For people, usually children, who sleep on the top bed of bunk beds, make sure that there are fixed secure railings so that they do not fall overboard.

Beds should have their headboards placed firmly against a wall to give some solid support. Some feng shui masters do not place high priority on this particular requirement and they state that it is acceptable to have space between the headboard and the wall behind if the head is pointed in an auspicious direction based on Eight Mansions feng shui (see Chapter 4.) My own feeling is that unless there is a solid wall behind, the sleeping person will be subject to unsettled, unstable, and inauspicious energy flow while he/she sleeps.

Bed placement with windows

Windows in the bedroom should ideally be by the side of the bed rather than behind the bed or directly in front of the bed. If the windows have to be behind the bed, they need to have curtains or blinds that can be securely closed during the night. Windows in front of the bed should also have a light transparent layer to diffuse excessively sharp energy coming in through the window directly at the bed. Those of you who can sleep with windows by the side of the bed benefit the most from benevolent fresh chi.

59

keeping things over
and under the bed

How you store items in the bedroom is also important. Anything that is stored over the bed, even books, can cause disturbed sleep. Under the bed is also a problem and is best kept clear.

It is not a good idea to have anything threatening or heavy above where you are sleeping, and especially over the top of your head. This can disturb chi when sleeping or make it unstable.

Books above the bed on shelves signify that the sleeping person is overwhelmed by new knowledge. If the sleeping person is a student, then this situation creates problems with their schoolwork. The student will experience stress and pressure and his/her work will start to suffer. Books should also never be kept under the bed – text books, notes, and essays that are handed in for marking purposes are particularly bad news. The symbolism of sleeping on your books and notes is like stepping over them, and this should be avoided at all costs. Instead, if you have to keep books in the bedroom, place them on side tables or on shelves that do not face the bed directly. Remember that books usually represent the acquisition of knowledge and this should never be compromised by bad feng shui.

Fans above the bed

Rotating ceiling fans directly above the bed are not recommended. In the old days when air conditioners had not yet been invented many expatriates and colonial officers who made their home in the tropical countries of Asia and Africa slept with fans directly above the bed. This usually brought about very bad luck. Indeed, fans above the bed represent very bad poison arrows coming at the bed and should be avoided. Instead, use table or floor fans.

Air conditioners should also not be placed directly above the bed or even on a side wall as the blast of cold air as well as the air-conditioner itself tend to create yin wind eddies inside the bedroom that can cause illness and sleepless nights. Ideally, place them on the floor or, if this is not possible, at least position them some way from the bed.

Precious items under the bed

Money, jewelry, and other precious things can be kept under the bed. This creates good money and prosperity luck for the person sleeping in the bed. When you sleep on top of precious jewels and money it signifies you are on top of these things. In fact, according to ritual feng shui, different types of precious stones can be placed under the bed to create various types of good luck and types of cures.

60

curing an afflicted multi-level bedroom

A split-level bedroom is quite a popular feature today, but care must be taken so that you position your bed on the upper level to ensure good relationships and happiness.

This kind of bedroom usually has the bed located on the lower or sunken level, and this is not a good bedroom arrangement. Even when there is only a single step separating the two levels, if you place the bed on the lower level it is symbolically inauspicious. This is because it is believed that sleeping on the lower level hurts all the relationships in your life, and there will be a tendency for people to take advantage of you. At work you will be ignored and, if your luck is really bad astrologically, you could even be made a scapegoat for all the bad things happening within your social and work circles.

Sleep on the higher level

So it is never a good idea to sleep on the lower level. If you really want a multi-level bedroom, then make sure you sleep on the upper level. If this is not possible, then do away with the two levels altogether or raise your bed so that you are at least higher than the higher level.

Sleeping on a lower level is always inauspicious. Note also that you must be careful where you place a wedding portrait. In this room it is directly facing the entrance door into the bedroom. This signifies that the marriage is being shown the exit door, and is not good for the couple occupying the room. In addition, the door of the toilet sends bad chi towards the bed.

61 dealing with a bedroom afflicted by a staircase

There are two ways a bedroom can be afflicted by the fast rising chi of a staircase. The first way is when the staircase directly faces the door into the bedroom.

It is always better for the staircase on the upper level to meet up with a wall than with a door.

A bed facing a staircase

The second way a staircase can create instability in the bedroom is when the bed is placed with the sleeping head directly pointing to a staircase going down. This symbolizes that your life is starting to go downhill. If this is a description that fits your bedroom you would be strongly advised to either move to another room or reposition the bed.

Staircases in apartments

If you live in an apartment block, it is a good idea to pay particular attention to outside common staircases as these can take on rather more ominous overtones than a single-storey staircase in homes. The outside staircases of apartments go down many levels, especially if you are living on a high floor. So if it is facing your bedroom door, then going downhill means taking a serious tumble in your affairs. Move your bed away from that wall, or better still move to another bedroom.

Sometimes, you may not realize that you are sleeping with your head pointed to a staircase, as shown here. Investigate if this is the case and if so, move your bed to another position; otherwise the symbolism of this arrangement means your life is going down hill.

62

solutions to L-shaped bedrooms

L-shaped bedrooms really need to be regularized and the way to do this depends on how much room you have to work with.

A re-planned L-shaped bedroom

The illustration below shows an L-shaped bedroom which has been laid out to regularize the sleeping area. A wall divider has been used to create a dressing area with a mirror which does not hurt the sleepers. Note that:

- The wall divider, which is also being used by the bed as the support wall, should be solid and firm. It does not need to be ceiling height but it does have to be solid enough to give real support to the bed.

- The dressing area behind the wall divider can have a mirror as the mirror will not be reflecting the bed. Mirrors that directly reflect the bed usually cause problems in the relationship between the sleeping couple. Mirrors in the bedroom are therefore considered to be a serious feng shui taboo. However, since the mirror in this example does not reflect the bed, it is acceptable.

- The location of the door into the bedroom makes the bed placement ideal inside the bedroom, because it is diagonally opposite the bed (see Tip 67.) However, please note that it directly faces the door into the toilet. So the former is a good feature, while the latter is a bad feature.

Compromising on feng shui principles

This example therefore shows how you can regularize the shape of your bedroom using a solid divider but, moreover, that it is not always possible to get everything a hundred percent right in the bedroom. Usually when it comes to doing the feng shui of your bedroom, or any room for that matter, it is usually a matter of compromising on some of the recommended features. In feng shui you have to weigh up your options, and then choose solutions that enable you to make the best of the practical realities facing you.

63

dealing with slanted and uneven ceilings

It is a fact of life that low, slanted, and uneven ceilings do not represent good feng shui. Low and uneven ceilings usually cause imbalance and create a feeling of being pressed down upon.

When you sleep on the side of the room where a sloping ceiling slopes down, the effect is also the same. Shar chi presses down on you as you sleep, and bad luck chi then accumulates around your person. To make matters worse, bedrooms with low or slanted ceilings are also very small and are often located high in the attic area of homes. The energy here is often depleted and unsteady. You should not place your son or daughter in such a bedroom as the affliction can cause them to suffer from bad luck, which builds up gradually over time and can be hard to shake off. If possible, move them out of such a bedroom. It is far better to use such rooms as storerooms.

Using attic bedrooms

However, if there is no choice and you need to sleep in this sort of undesirable bedroom, I would strongly recommend that a series of low voltage lights are placed on the ceiling itself to symbolically raise the energy of the ceiling. The room should also be cleverly painted to make it seem rather more vertical than horizontal, so use lightly differentiated vertical colors. Lighter colors also work better than darker colors. If possible, install a

window in the room that brings in some light, as the presence of fresh yang energy (especially of natural sunlight) will greatly improve the feng shui of the room.

Flat ceilings are auspicious

Meanwhile, please do note that flat ceilings, which are safe and well balanced, are best. Never have anything that is sharp or threatening pointing down from the ceiling onto the bed as over time this can cause illness.

Bedrooms in the loft with sloping ceilings are not really suitable for children as the energy can be unbalanced.

64 have balanced lighting in the bedroom

Bedroom lighting should never be excessively bright as this can create yang energy that becomes harsh and hurtful in a bedroom, so I do not recommend crystal chandeliers or track spotlights here.

Overhead lights should always be evenly spaced out. These should be small, of low voltage, and the perfect number to have of such recessed ceiling lights is six, which is the number for heaven.

It is also a good idea if just directly above the bed are placed two lights that are nicely balanced on either side of the bed.

If you only want to have one light then having it on the dragon or left side of the bed is better than on the tiger or right side. However, nothing beats balance in feng shui, so having the lights on both sides of the bed is really the best situation as this symbolically offers the success luck brought by the dragon and also the protective luck brought by the tiger.

65 princess beds and full-canopied beds

Elaborate and romantic beds that have either full or half canopies attract mixed views from different feng shui masters.

Some say such beds bring good feng shui as they are protective and reminiscent of the womb environment, while others maintain that beds like these signify being imprisoned.

I tend to go with the former view as these remind me of princess beds, which suggest a certain luxury. So, I simply have to think of them as being auspicious. Princess beds are those with a half canopy with a beautiful soft material. The canopy does not harm the sleeping person below.

Full-canopied beds enjoy excellent feng shui. Such beds are usually associated with kings and powerful people. Beds like these are well balanced and more than adequately protected. They give a feeling of security, providing those who occupy them with good, uninterrupted sleep.

66 the effect of different headboards

I have often been asked about the feng shui of bed headboards, and my answer has always been that beds with headboards have better feng shui than beds without them.

This is because apart from symbolizing completeness for the bed, headboards also offer some support for the sleeping person. However, there is room for creativity in using different kinds of headboards. The difference can be made in the shape, the materials used, the colors, and the designs. Generally speaking, wooden and fabric headboards that offer solid but soft support offer the best potential for a good night's sleep and accumulation of healthy positive chi energy. Brass or iron headboards usually have holes between their spokes and these offer little support, and do not do much to help the accumulation of chi.

Headboard shapes for good and bad feng shui

semi-circular

A headboard with a semi-circular upward protrusion represents good feng shui, but the semi circle does give the suggestion of incompleteness.

turtle-shaped

A headboard that has a turtle-shaped appearance looks better on a double bed. On a single bed it resembles a tombstone and is therefore not favored by the Chinese.

rectangular

A rectangular headboard represents the wood element and signifies robust and healthy growth. This kind of headboard is balanced and particularly well suited for growing children.

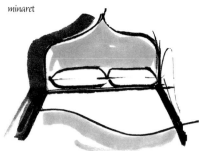

minaret

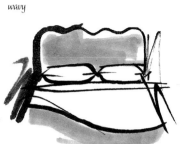

wavy

triangular

A headboard that has a minaret shape is best avoided as it is believed to cause problems associated with the limbs. This form also suggests the Fire Element, and sleeping with Fire behind you is certainly bad feng shui.

A wavy headboard signifies the Water Element; it is neither good nor bad.

slatted

A headboard that has a triangular shape is said to represent the Fire Element. This is excellent to use if you are in short supply of yang energy, i.e. if you are lacking energy, seem listless, or don't do enough exercise. But you should nevertheless be wary of this kind of headboard as Fire energy when sleeping can turn malevolent.

A slatted headboard looks like a ladder, which brings bad luck. Such headboards are best avoided, as they are thought to be unstable.

Other shapes

Slanting headboards should be gently curving and the man should sleep on the higher dragon side. When you have a bed with this sort of headboard, it is also sometimes referred to as the dragon and phoenix bed and they can be lucky and harmonious when the male is the major breadwinner in the household and this is the bed in the main, master bedroom.

If the woman of the partnership also has a career, this headboard could cause unconscious competition between the couple and instead of a dragon and phoenix the chi of two dragons is created, which makes the energy unbalanced.

Fan-shaped headboards are more decorative, and can take different styles and patterns. From a feng shui perspective these headboards are acceptable as long as they are properly balanced. A fan-shaped headboard tends to be excellent for growing children, especially daughters, as they tend to have protective chi. When the daughters grow up decorative, fan-shaped headboards bring good marriage opportunities.

67 good and bad room layouts

How you place bedroom furniture is almost exclusively determined by the position of the bed. So bedroom layouts are good or bad depending on where and how the bed is placed.

While it is necessary to observe all the bedroom taboos, and thought must be given to where toilets are positioned in the home or on other floors, there are also basic guidelines governing the best and worst positions of the bed in the bedroom layout.

The best bedroom layout

A good bedroom design is always where the bed(s) are placed in the far corner of the room, diagonally opposite to the door (see illustration below.) This allows the sleeping person a full view

Good bedroom layouts mean positioning your bed so that it is diagonally opposite the bedroom door. The door should not cut into any of the bed, which would cause negative chi to rush towards the sleeper.

of the door, so that they are not surprised by any sudden entrances through the door. It does not matter where the head is pointing, as long as the placement of the bed itself follows the natural shape of the bedroom.

A bad bedroom layout

Bad bedroom arrangements create sleeping problems for those who occupy the room. They will get very restless and find it hard to get a good night's sleep, but what is equally significant is that they will also suffer the consequences of a bad feng shui layout. A bad bedroom layout occurs when a door opening into the bedroom cuts directly into the bed, or when the bed is somehow directly aligned with the door so that the sleeping person has either their feet or their head pointing towards the door.

This is often described as the death position – with head or legs pointed directly at the door, as this is the way people who have died are carried out. This position is banned in hospitals and the Chinese are very against this way of sleeping. They always make certain this particular taboo of bedroom feng shui is never, ever broken as they consider it such bad luck.

Sleeping with your feet pointing towards the door (far left) is known as the death position, so is always thought to be inauspicious. Any bed position that means the door opens onto the side of the bed or close to the bed head is not good feng shui. This is because cutting chi symbolically harms the bed and therefore its occupants.

68 good layouts for the dining room

The best place for the dining room is in the center of the home as this strengthens its importance in the household. However, if it is too near the front door, the family's wealth can be affected.

The dining room is the room where the family gathers to eat, and this creates two major feng shui implications. Firstly, it determines the overall family luck and affects the way family members interact and cooperate with each other, and secondly the dining room also influences the family's ability to sustain and maintain its fortunes and wealth. So the dining room is a very important room in the home.

Dine in the center of the home

Ideally, the dining room should be located in the center of the home so that it represents the heart of the home. This enhances and magnifies its importance within the household. It also strengthens the importance of the family unit, and creates the kind of feng shui that ensures that the family stay together.

The dining room should never be too near the front door into the home as it can cause family wealth to dissipate and literally flow out of the door.

Bad positioning

It should never be positioned in such a way that the dining table itself faces a toilet as this will create health problems. If your dining room is placed like this, try to obscure the view of the toilet with

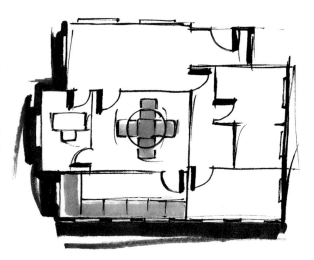

When the dining room is in the center of the home the family stays intact and together. When dining rooms are too near the front door, residents tend to be undisciplined about their work. Too near the dragon or tiger sides is also not a good idea. The center enhances the family's positive sentiments.

a curtain or some other form of concealing divider.

The dining room is more auspicious when it is placed in the inner half of the home, as this will ensure that the family's wealth stays intact, and does not flow out easily.

Dining rooms should always be higher, or on an equal level with the living room. When there are multiple levels in the home, it is always considered more auspicious to locate the dining room on the higher level.

69 how to position the dining table

It is important to focus your energy on making sure that the placement of dining tables is correct and therefore conducive to good feng shui.

To start with do invest in an auspicious dining table (see Tip 34.) Make certain that the surface area of the table is large enough. Generally speaking, larger tables tend to create better feng shui than smaller tables. Dining tables can be made of wood or glass, be circular or rectangular, and are best when standing on a single large and solid leg if they are round. This is because it is believed that the table then resembles a wealth tree, a fortuitous symbol for the Chinese. Rectangular dining tables should be large enough to have six auspicious legs, or even eight super auspicious legs!

The correct position

When the dining table and chairs have been selected the next step is to position the dining table correctly.

When the dining table is placed between two doors the chi created is not good. It is better to move the table out of the line of fire, otherwise there will be what is termed "bullfighting shar chi." If you have no choice but to use this sort of dining table placement, then I strongly recommend that you hang windchimes somewhere near the table, between it and the door. This should slow down the chi and reduce some of the negative effect. If one of the doors is opposite a toilet door, it is not a bad idea to place a full-length mirror on the door into the toilet, as this has the effect of making it symbolically disappear.

Placed under a beam

If the dining table is placed directly beneath an exposed overhead beam, then anyone sitting there will have his/her luck pressed down upon. It is not a good situation as in time the pressure can cause migraines and headaches, and general health can be badly affected. It is much better to move the table to a less threatening position, away from under the beam.

When the dining table is placed in a small tight corner and the rest of the home is spacious and prominent, this signifies that the family is being squeezed out of the house. The feng shui created is simply not good and efforts should be made to redesign the layout so that more space is given to the dining room area.

Also do not position dining tables between two pillars. Alternatively, use some plants and windchimes as an effective remedy.

When a dining table can be seen from the main door, then you need to place a divider in between so that the view is obscured. Otherwise the symbolism is that money simply flows out and the family soon loses its wealth.

Remedies for bad table positions

Placing the table directly between two doors is like placing the family's rice bowl in the line of fire. Close one door permanently, or move the dining table to the side.

Here the table is being cut in half by an exposed overhead beam; this will cause the family to argue and have disagreements around the table. Use a false ceiling to camouflage the beam or use another room for family dining.

When the dining room is too near to the toilet, keep the toilet door closed or hang a curtain embroidered or printed with auspicious objects.

70 feng shui rules on kitchens

The feng shui of kitchens has important and significant implications for the luck of the household. It can also affect the wealth of the residents.

This is especially so when the family eats at home more than it eats out. It is also correct to say that when the kitchen has good energy, which is maintained, then the family will prefer to eat in rather than out.

A good kitchen brings prosperity

The kitchen feng shui also affects the wealth of the family. When it is properly located in the inner half of the home, preferably on the ground floor, and its location does not upset any of the feng shui intangible forces related to formula feng shui, then the kitchen can not only attract prosperity for the family, but also protect it from loss situations developing and bringing bad luck.

The ideal placement

Kitchens should ideally never be located in the center of the home, and certainly never in the northwest as this represents fire at heaven's gate. Their best location is either right at the back of the home or situated on one side of the home. If the house also has a basement level, the kitchen must not be located down there as this will cause serious hurt or misfortune to befall the matriarch of the family.

For those who follow Eight Mansions feng shui, please note that your kitchen should be located in one of your inauspicious sectors. This is because the kitchen has the power to press down on severe bad luck areas.

The best location for a kitchen is towards the back of the home, on the ground floor.

71 positioning your kitchen stove

Although the kitchen can be located in one of the inauspicious sectors of the home, based on compass feng shui formula, the family stove must be placed in an auspicious direction.

It is even more important to note that the energy fuelling the stove needs to come from your best direction. This direction is never immediately obvious, so examine the gas or electricity inflow carefully. A simpler method is to ensure that your rice cooker (stove), kettle, and toaster all have their plug inlets facing the best direction.

Position the stove diagonally opposite the door, and away from the sink.

Inauspicious positions

An additional rule for positioning the stove is that it should never face the main door as this symbolizes a loss of livelihood, causing the breadwinner to lose his or her job. So this is a serious affliction and the stove must be repositioned – no matter how difficult it is to do. Otherwise, when the astrological period of the house is low, or when the flying stars coming into the house turn bad, then loss of income or livelihood will be bad. The negativity coming from this may be irreversible.

Bad effects from above

It is also vital to protect the stove from any bad energy coming down from above. The worst effect is when the stove is directly under a toilet from the upper floor. Not so harmful, but also negative, is when the water tank is situated directly above the stove. This causes water and fire confrontation, bringing commotion and quarrels in the home. Also beware of anything that is too heavy that is directly above the kitchen stove. This could be a structural beam, a bed, cupboard, bath, or shower.

A window directly above the stove can adversely affect the stove and may bring instability of employment. Also avoid mirrors or mirror tiles above the cooker or anywhere in the kitchen. This is because they do not double the food being cooked, but instead are dangerous, doubling the fire effect.

To prevent more bad feng shui, make sure the stove does not face a staircase, a refrigerator, a toilet, a store room, a door, or a water pipe. The best position for the stove is diagonally opposite the kitchen door, as illustrated. But if it is then hit by the back door, put a divider there to block the energy coming from the door. Finally, stoves must never be placed too near a sink as the Fire Element will react negatively to the Water Element.

72   toilets and the problems they cause

Toilets in any part of the home always cause problems, so I am constantly encouraging people to have small toilets that are conveniently tucked away.

If you can do this, it makes the problem of the energy created by toilets easier to control. If this is not possible, then the most practical way to handle them is to systematically dissolve or dissipate bad toilet energy.

Re-planning toilet doors

The most effective way of handling toilets is to reposition their doors so that they do not confront other doors and bring about misfortunes. So if the toilet door faces the main door, the symbolism is that wealth simply gets carried away. In this case, reposition the toilet door, or paint it bright red.

Bad positioning for the toilet

These other locations of the toilet can adversely affect the home.

- Toilets that face the living room create a negative effect on social life and friendships, so again reposition the toilet door if you can.
- When the toilet door faces the dining room it means having a hard time professionally, and the family can quarrel. The solution is to create some barrier that blocks off the view of the toilet. When it is on the other side of a wall shared with the dining table it causes loss of livelihood.

If the toilet door faces the living room door, symbolically make it disappear by hanging a mirror or curtain over it.

- If the toilet is above a main door, shine a light upwards to symbolically deflect the bad energy.
- If the toilet shares a wall with a study and the desk is on the other side, it can cause bad luck while working.
- When the toilet is sharing a wall with an aquarium on the other side, it can bring about loss of wealth.
- When a dressing table is on the other side, it can affect your looks.

Dispersing bad toilet energy

There are several ways to counteract the negative energy of toilets. You can place a bright light inside the toilet to introduce strong yang energy. Alternatively, paint the door of the toilet a bright red; however, this is rather drastic. You can also put a mirror on the outside of the toilet door. This visually, and symbolically, makes it "disappear."

73

installing aquariums for prosperity

One of the most popular methods that Chinese businessmen who believe in feng shui use to attract prosperity to their companies, is installing aquariums.

Indeed the keeping of live fish in aquariums is one of the easiest feng shui basics to have in the home. The most popular fish kept are the many varieties of goldfish, the dragon fish (also referred to as the silver or golden arrowana,) and carp (Japanese koi fish.) These three varieties of fish are believed to signify great abundance and prosperity luck. Keeping them in bubbling water gives the added dimension of yang water which is itself also an energizer of good fortune. This kind of water is an ideal energizer since it is activated in a controlled environment and the water itself is alive, but small enough not to be overwhelming.

Placing aquariums or small ponds

Aquariums or small ponds that contain any of the three varieties of fish mentioned above could be regarded as one of the basic features to have in your home if you want to use feng shui to activate wealth luck. There is, of course, a correct and not-so-correct way to display aquariums. To start with they should really only be kept in the north, east, or southeast of the living room to be safe – if you do not know the more advanced ways of figuring out the best location. If you place the aquarium in any of these three designated corners of the living room you will not go wrong. Use a compass to work out these corners. Remember that you are

keeping an aquarium to attract the luck of abundance, wealth, and success, and so it is worthwhile ensuring the aquarium water is kept clean, and that the fish are healthy and are neither overfed nor left to starve. Sometimes the first batch of fish may die. This is because the ph balance in the water has not yet settled down. This is unfortunate, but keep trying. Soon the water will settle and your fish will be happy. Another excellent corner for aquariums or small indoor fish ponds is where the auspicious water star eight is in your home. To discover where this is you need to understand flying star feng shui as the water star eight is in different corners of the home, depending on several factors that influence the natal chart of houses. Please try to get hold of my book on flying star feng shui to work this out. In the meantime, use the corners I have suggested here. You should notice a difference in your money luck soon after you have positioned it.

Inauspicious locations

Do not let the aquarium face the front door as the effect it causes is like a mirror, and this indicates your wealth flowing out of the house. Also, do not use the aquarium as a divider between two doors, as this will only make a bad situation worse. Never place aquariums in the kitchen, under a beam, facing a toilet, or under a staircase.

74 feng shui fish bring prosperity

In feng shui, fish are potent activators of wealth luck. The most auspicious fish are those which are gold or red in color, representing money.

One of the most powerful and beautiful feng shui fish to keep is the dragon fish, or arrowana. If you cannot find them, choose gold-fish or guppies; their rippling movement represents precious yang energy, and their presence in your home welcomes in prosperity. Always have nine fish, or multiples of nine, including a single black fish. This is because the black fish symbolically absorbs any negative chi that enters the surrounding space. Also, do not be disheartened if one or more of your fish dies – you have not inadvertently created bad fortune for yourself. Replace your fish if you need to, and always keep their living conditions clean and cared for. This encourages the best flow of chi within the tank, ensuring that money flows to you, rather than out of your home. For this reason, never keep an aquarium by your main door, and observe bedroom taboos: fish tanks in bedrooms disturb the natural yin energy of this room and cause relationship problems.

75 using six-rod chimes for five yellow affliction

To control the bad luck of the five yellow affliction, a windchime is especially effective, and for this purpose a six-rod windchime is the most powerful.

The windchime should be all-metal, with round and hollow rods and, if possible, it should emit a sharp tinkling sound when the rods strike against each other. Five-rod chimes can also be used but they are not as powerful as the six-rod variety. The sound of metal on metal will dissolve and exhaust all the negative energy that is in the room, or the corners affected. In 2001 the five yellow affliction will reside in the southwest, so this corner of your home should have a windchime. To discover where the five yellow affliction will be in each new year please refer to www.wofs.com.

76 using windchimes as feng shui remedies

Probably one of the most effective and powerful cures in feng shui is using a windchime. In fact, if you want to practice feng shui well you should be familiar with the use (and misuse) of windchimes.

Always remember that windchimes are one of the best remedies for dissolving harmful negative energy caused by the intangible and invisible effect of bad stars that fly in and out of living spaces bringing havoc, misfortune, and accidents wherever they temporarily settle. These are said to be the stars that represent what is colorfully referred to as the stars that bring the five yellow ghosts and the three killings chi. Each year these harmful stars make their home in different corners of the house and wherever they settle in that year they bring bad luck. If the corner they settle in happens to be where your front door is placed, the whole house can suffer from misfortunes, accidents, and ill health during that year. And if they settle in your bedroom then you will feel the full brunt of the misfortunes luck.

Metal windchimes are wonderful protectors, and are great for energizing the northwest and west sectors. Wooden chimes are less effective.

Windchimes for protection

Much like a sentinel, windchimes can be hung up in quiet corners to guard against the emergence of any kind of intangible, harmful chi. This will ensure that even though you may not be familiar with the more advanced formulas of feng shui you will nevertheless have taken feng shui insurance by having your all-metal windchime hung up in place. However, when you do use a windchime, do note the following guidelines:

- Never sit directly under a windchime.

- Never hang it directly above a door or doorway.

- Hang it near a flow of breeze; by a window is best.

Windchimes are also excellent for correcting:

- Protruding corners and overhead beams.

- Two or three doors in a straight line.

- Doors that face a toilet, staircase, balcony, or other inauspicious feature.

77 Neutralizing overhead beams

One of the most basic problems encountered by everyone in the course of their feng shui practice is the problem caused by exposed overhead beams.

The worst kinds of beams are the heavy structural beams which can be extremely harmful in high-rise apartment buildings, or in low-cost apartment blocks where construction budgets simply do not allow for the beams to be hidden away in the walls. So exposed beams are a feng shui problem that is encountered in varying degrees by everyone.

Beams in old properties

Beams are also a problem when you live in old houses that have no ceilings, because the supporting beams are all exposed. I did spend one horrible night without sleep in such a room, and it is definitely no fun. I discovered that every member of the family in that household suffered from severe migraines and had been suffering the problem for so long that they had learnt to live with it! I recommended that they installed a false ceiling to visually block off the beams. They did just that and not only did they get rid of their headaches, but they also vastly improved their luck.

The most harmful beams are the heavy, exposed structural ones. Rectangular beams made of concrete and steel with sharp edges are more harmful than smaller round wooden beams. These exposed beams need to be dealt with, especially when they are found at entrances, above desk and tables, cut-ting across beds and dining tables, and in living areas. To start with, arrange your furniture – beds, tables, sofa sets, and chairs – in such a way that they are not directly under an exposed beam. No matter what you do to alleviate the hostile chi from these beams emanating downwards and hitting you, you will still be affected to some extent. The question is only how severe this negative chi will be. So move any furniture out from under them.

Dealing with exposed beams

There are different ways of dealing with exposed beams. You can install a false plaster or wood ceiling to disguise the beam, or hang two hollow bamboo flutes tied with red ribbons at the edge of the beams. Hang the two pieces of bamboo slanting towards each other. This transforms the hostile energy into harmless energy. It is also possible to use lighting and paint to camouflage the effect of heavy-looking overhead beams. Lights can overcome hostile energy, so use bright crystal lights to burn away the bad energies emanating from these beams.

A final cure, possibly the most powerful, is the symbolic remedy of hanging a red firecracker to blast away the beam. This is not very effective against structural beams so install mirrors around the beams to symbolically make them disappear.

3

applying the

five elements

to enhance the

chi of the home

78 five energies influence the chi of the home

The Chinese believe that everything in the Universe is made up of five Elements which are described as five types of chi energy – Earth, Water, Wood, Metal, and Fire.

These five types of chi continuously interact with each other in a circular destructive, productive, and exhaustive relationship. Understanding these interactions in the context of space and time dimensions enables the feng shui practitioner to manipulate the way energy manifests good and bad luck in the any living and work space.

Understanding the Five Elements

To become really effective at practical feng shui you must understand the essence of these five types of energy. This is because everything in the Universe, and therefore all the structures, shapes,

Water energy is flowing and fluid. It brings wealth and success.

The Fire Element is yang, meaning bright and very active energy. It brings life and progress.

colors, and orientations of your home, contains either one or a combination of the Five Element connotations. So seasons, colors, shapes, directions of energy flows, and even numbers have Element equivalents. Learning how the chi of the different Elements interact with each other, and how their attributes manifest in each corner of the home, will enable you to produce great feng shui energy in your home. It will also give you the remedies to control, exhaust, and even destroy bad chi, which brings bad luck. The Five Elements is therefore an invaluable dimension for creating great feng shui.

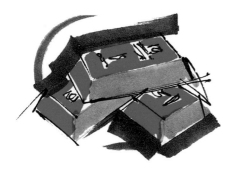

Metal energy is rigid and cold. It brings value and prosperity.

need to learn is that the cardinal and secondary directions of the compass each have a corresponding Element. The easiest way to create good feng shui is to find out what kind of Element is best for your home, and how you can strengthen it. At the same time you need to become extremely wary of having too strong a presence of Elements that will hurt your home. This has implications in your use of color, in the placement of objects, and even in your choice of rooms for yourself and family members.

At the same time even your home or building has an intrinsic Element energy, and if you are able to identify the Element of your home you are already in a position to do something to enhance its energy in a most spectacular way. Once you know your home's Element, activating it for good luck becomes a piece of cake.

With knowledge of the attributes of the Elements and how they influence each of the eight sectors of the compass, feng shui practice becomes easy and fun. Why? Because all you

Earth energy is all-encompassing. It brings love and family relationships.

Energizing different areas

You can also energize the Element of each compass sector of the individual rooms within the home as well. Once you have strengthened each of the Elements in all the eight corners of your home, it will vibrate with positive and strong energy. So understanding the five chi energies is a central part of feng shui practice – simply by understanding each of the Five Elements you can create great feng shui.

Wood energy is green and alive. It brings growth.

79 working out the element of your home

Every building has a trigram and Element that governs the nature of its chi attributes. To discover your home's Element, you need to find how it is sited, which is derived from its orientation.

This is your homes "sitting" direction, which is opposite to its facing direction. So the first thing you need to do is stand at the main front door of your home, then, looking out, point a compass directly in front of you to determine the direction that your home faces. This direction must be taken at the door and it should be as accurate as possible. Learn to read and use a compass, because almost all genuine Chinese feng shui practice and recommendations are based on compass directions.

How to work out the directions

Also, when we refer to any of the directions we are really referring to the directions based on north being the magnetic north of the western compass. So you can use a western compass in your feng shui practice. All feng shui recommendations apply equally for countries in the Northern and Southern hemispheres.

If your home faces east, your sitting direction will be west (this is because in feng shui terms the sitting direction is opposite the facing direction.) This enables you to quickly work out the sitting direction of your home. Those living in apartments should use the entrance into the apartment block to get the sitting direction of the whole apartment building.

Working out your home's Element

- **If your sitting direction is north, then the governing Element is Water.**

- **If the sitting direction is south, then the governing Element is Fire.**

- **If your sitting direction is east or southeast the governing Element is Wood.**

- **If the sitting direction is west or northwest, the governing Element is Metal.**

- **If the sitting direction is southwest or northeast the governing Element is Earth.**

There are different ways you can enhance, strengthen, and support the Element of your house and building. One very effective way is to use color combinations – so for Water houses, use combinations of white (because Metal produces Water) and blue; for Fire houses use warm color combinations of yellow and red; for Wood houses use blue or black (because Water produces Wood) with green; for Metal houses use yellow (because Earth produces Metal) with white; while for Earth houses use red (because Fire produces Earth) with yellow.

80

differentiating between small chi and big chi

One of the great secrets of practical feng shui is knowing the difference between small chi and big chi. This is valid irrespective of whether you are using formula or form school feng shui.

In theory what this means is that you can apply feng shui to individual rooms of a home or to the home itself. When you are looking at individual rooms this signifies activating small chi, while the house chi is referred to as big chi.

The eastern sector

So when we speak of placing a dragon image in the east, we are referring to placing it in the eastern sector of the entire house. However, it could also be placed in the eastern sector of individual rooms to enhance the small chi. The good and bad effect of enhancers or harmful objects stays equal in strength and potency, whether or not you are applying small or big chi. This fact is a small, but extremely significant clarification, which I sought from Taoist feng shui masters – and they were in agreement. They revealed emphatically that energy is relative, whether auspicious or unlucky, so, for example, the small chi of any corner of a room is as potent as the big chi of the same corner of the whole house.

A southwest affliction

This means that when the southwest of your home is afflicted by a toilet, or is missing, and you worry about the negative effects on your love life,

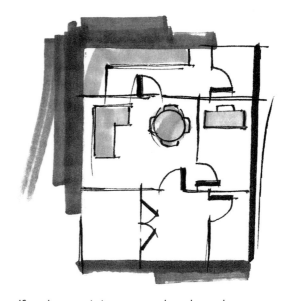

If you have a missing corner, such as the southwest, you can activate the "small chi" by enhancing the southwest corner of other rooms.

you can decide to strongly enhance the small chi of the southwest corner of your bedroom, or any room that you frequently use, instead. This should bring back good energy into the southwest, and override its affliction.

You can also activate your auspicious sheng chi direction (see Tip 110) by enhancing that particular sector of your whole house, or just by focusing on the living room. The potency of a feng shui energizer depends on how much you use the enhanced space, rather than its size.

81

the two cycles of element interaction

The two cycles that define the way Elements interact with each other are an indispensable tool in feng shui practice. The cycles are productive and destructive.

Basically, almost all of feng shui practice requires an understanding of these two cycles. It is the correct manipulation of the strength or weakness of the Element energy within a space that enables us to enhance the chi there, or to overcome and weaken afflicted chi.

The Productive and Destructive cycles

The first stage of Element interaction lies in the two major cycles – the Productive and Destructive.

The Productive Cycle works like this in a "feeding" cycle: Water produces Wood, Wood produces Fire, Fire produces Earth, Earth produces Metal, and Metal produces Water.

The Productive Cycle offers powerful pointers on how to enhance any of the Five Elements by using the Element that produces it. So to enhance Wood we use Water because Water produces Wood; to enhance Metal we use Earth because Earth produces Metal, and so forth.

So to enhance the chi of any sector of the house or room, we first need to check the compass sector and its Element, then we can apply the productive Element.

The north sector is Water, so use a metal object to enhance this corner; the south sector is Fire so use a wooden item to enhance this corner; the east and southeast sectors are Wood so use water accessories to enhance; the west and northwest are Metal so use earth – ceramics or crystals – to enhance; and finally the southwest and northeast are Earth so use fire objects such as lights or candles to enhance.

In the Destructive Cycle, Water destroys Fire, Fire destroys Metal, Metal destroys Wood, Wood destroys Earth, and Earth destroys Water.

The Destructive Cycle offers strong ways to overcome and even destroy any one of the Five Elements that may be afflicted, by using the Element that destroys it. To control bad Wood energy use Metal because Metal destroys Wood; to overcome afflicted Metal chi use Fire because Fire destroys Metal, and so forth. So to enhance the chi of any sector, check to see which compass sector you're dealing with and its Element, so that you can apply the destructive Element.

So for an afflicted north, Water, sector use Earth (ceramics and crystals) to overcome; for an afflicted southern, Fire, sector use Water items to overcome; for afflicted east and southeast, Wood, sectors use Metal accessories to overcome; for afflicted west and northwest, Metal, sectors use Fire (lighting and candles) to overcome; and for afflicted southwest and northeast, Earth, sectors use wooden objects as remedies.

85 jump-start relationships with fire chi

Fire energy is especially great for jump-starting luck in the relationship areas of your home. The Element of the relationship sector is K'un, or Earth, which can be strengthened with Fire chi.

If your knowledge of feng shui does not extend to the powerful Eight Mansions or flying star formula you can simply consider the southwest corner of your home, or rooms, to be the areas that represent your relationship luck. Feng shui does not have to be difficult or complex for it to work. All the formulas complement and strengthen each other. They do not replace one another, nor is there a ranking as to potency and speed in seeing results.

Locating southwest sectors

To find the southwest sector, use a good orienteering compass to get its direction. Remember that directions do not exist on their own.

Directions are always expressed in terms of a point of reference. So stand in the center of your room to identify the southwest corner, and stand in the center of the home to identify its southwest corner. This sector signifies the trigram K'un, which is of the big Earth Element. Activate this energy with plenty of Fire energy. Put crystal lights and red lamps here to create potently powerful yang energy, and everyone will benefit from a smoother ride in their relationships. At work – with colleagues, bosses, and subordinates – and most importantly with loved ones, a well-energized K'un sector brings happier interactions. Social life improves and friendships take on deeper meanings. Love also gets activated for those in search of meaningful relationships.

Red lamps and crystals in the southwest create yang energy, which boosts relationships.

86

fine-tuning your relationship feng shui

If you are keen to go further in your feng shui practice, you can use the Eight Mansions formula to identify your personalized directions for love, health, relationships, and personal development.

For this formula please refer to Tip 110 in Chapter 4 on Eight Mansions applications. The formula will reveal what direction is best for you to activate your relationship luck. This direction is known as the Nien Yen, and it is based on your Kua number calculated from your date of birth and gender. Depending on which sector is specified as being your relationship and love sector, you should activate the Element of this sector. Fire energy is used only if your personalized relationship sector is the southwest or the northeast – both Earth sectors. Note that it is better to use the Element that produces the sector's Element, rather than the Element itself. Refer back to the productive Cycle of Elements in Tip 79 to discover which Elements to use.

Utilizing flying star feng shui

If you know about flying star feng shui you can fine-tune the relationships sector even further, complementing your energizing of the southwest and your personalized Kua direction. Flying star feng shui affects all the residents equally. It is not personalized according to individuals. It uses the natal chart of buildings (which includes houses) and these are based on the attributes of them, although bear in mind that this comes into a more advanced study of feng shui.

But you can activate the sectors of your house or rooms where there are auspicious relationships stars by following the table given in the flying star section of this book (see Tips 182–187,) where I have worked out the sectors for all houses built or renovated on or after the 4th February 1984, and which will apply to houses built or renovated up to February 4th 2004.

These charts are based on the orientation of your home, which means the outward facing direction of the main front door. Those who live in apartments should use the building's main entrance as their point of reference. Please remember that this table contains simplified flying star applications for those who do not know flying star feng shui!

Taking compass directions

This is the only book where such tables have been summarized. The auspicious relationship sector will be the sectors indicated by the directions stated against the door facing directions. When you are taking the directions indicated in the tables, always use a proper compass for accuracy of your home's orientation. Feng shui uses these compass directions to manipulate the intangible energy or chi of our space, so please use a compass.

87

fire to boost luck in examinations

Fire is an excellent energizer of the chi of knowledge and wisdom. Based on the Pa Kua method, the direction which stands for knowledge is the northeast.

Simply strengthening the Element of your northeast corner or room will help the knowledge chi of the home to accumulate. This brings excellent luck for those residents who may be taking examinations at school or at college. It also helps anyone who does research activities or who may be engaged in serious meditation work. The Element of the northeast is Earth and, as Fire produces Earth in the productive Cycle of Elements, the essence of Fire energy is extremely nourishing to expand this luck.

Burning incense in the northeast corner brings knowledge luck.

Enhancing the northeast

So when you study, work or meditate, place a small lighted candle on a table in the northeast corner of the room you are using. The same effect can also be created by burning some incense. This simulates the actual creation of Earth by the Fire energy because burning the incense creates ash. It is for this reason that many traditions use the burning of incense in their various rituals. It is excellent for engaging the chi energy of the surrounding space and enhancing its potency.

The Chinese are very fond of burning sandalwood incense and this is a ritual that has been recommended for centuries for scholars who study into the night. You can also use a special herbal or pine incense to assist in meditation.

Finding your northeast corner

If your northeast is not available, because there is a toilet located there or it is missing due to the shape of your home, then try to study and work in another room where this corner is available.

You can also identify the most auspicious corner of the room for studying under flying star feng shui. However, learning the advanced flying star feng shui is rather complex. So for generating knowledge and examination luck use the Pa Kua method described here, or the Eight Mansions method (see Tip 110) which specifies your auspicious directions based on your year of birth and gender, to activate luck that favors personal development. If your auspicious direction is not northeast or southwest, don't use Fire energy.

88 fire energy should not be too strong

In feng shui, Fire energy is considered a double-edged sword. It is a strong and passionate Element that brings roaring recognition and success.

However, it also has the potential to hurt when it reaches its zenith and has got out of control. At its worst fire burns and kills, yet at its best Fire energy brings global acknowledgement of your brilliance and honor. Politicians, and all those of you engaged in professions requiring public recognition especially, have the potential to either benefit strongly or get badly burnt by the Element of Fire.

But the big secret in application is to never allow Fire to get out of control, so do not activate it too strongly. Remember at all times that Fire is very powerful, as it is the ultimate yang Element. Too much Fire brings excessive yang energy, which is just as harmful as insufficient yang. When yin is completely missing, yang ceases to exist.

Fire needs to be created

Fire itself does not exist on its own; it needs to be created. Unlike other Elements, it cannot be stored. So each time you want to use Fire chi you have to create it. Its essence, however, can be generated with light symbols, which are less likely to be excessive. It is only when you create naked flames that the danger of excessive Fire exists, so do be careful when burning candles.

Too many lights

When you use bright lights, don't use so many that you change your corner into a blinding film studio setting. For the same reason do not light so many candles that you create the danger of one of them falling over and starting a real fire. If you activate with red colors, do not have so much that the excess yang energy turns malevolent instead of staying benign and benevolent. When it comes to using Fire energy to activate corners always temper how much you use.

Hanging red lanterns stimulates Fire chi in a controlled way, unlike naked flames, which can generate excessive Fire chi.

89

the challenge of the water element

Water chi is the Element of wealth, but like Fire it can get out of control. Water energy moves downwards, so when it overflows it has the potential to create massive bad luck.

The *I Ching* strenuously warns against water at its zenith – when it is at a high point. Because water flows downwards, this creates a situation of extreme danger, and feng shui recognizes this danger, so it always warns against having big pools of water at the very top of multi-storey buildings. Blue and black, the colors which represent the Water Element, are also never recommended for rooftops or even as color schemes for apartments that are located on the highest floor. Also remember that overflowing water suggests loss of wealth and the source of wealth, and possible danger.

Water can bring success

Water brings prosperity when it is energized correctly and in the right amounts. Water in feng shui links to the north and its trigram Kan. So when you place a water feature in the north corner of your home or any rooms (except the bedroom) water brings in good luck. I have also calculated the flying stars for this and the next periods 7 and 8, which according to my calculations north will benefit from the presence of water features filled with yang water. This brings continued wealth luck. As before, this can be the north of your house, individual rooms, or even the north of your garden.

This apartment's main door faces north. Placing water here is auspicious.

Activating the north

When you activate your chosen northern areas, do use a compass to identify these corners accurately, and also take note and observe the feng shui taboos and guidelines regarding the use of water and you will guard against creating other problems as you activate these wealth areas. In feng shui sometimes a little knowledge can be a dangerous thing, so do endeavour to be careful when activating your corners, especially when using Water chi.

90 best corners for water inside the home

If you know how to tap Water chi correctly you will know the secret of using feng shui to attract wealth luck. All the formulas address the question of water.

In fact I have discovered that this is probably the easiest type of chi to activate. There are several different formulas that offer advice on the best corners for placing water, and I shall summarize all the different methods for you. What you should do first is investigate the constraints imposed by your particular living situation, then select the corner that means something good based on each of the different methods of activating water.

Good water corners

All the different methods of identifying the lucky water corners work, but how much wealth luck they generate for you will depend on your own luck. So for some of you, once you activate water correctly you could well come into a windfall that brings in lots of money, while for others it could manifest as a good raise at work, some extra income coming in from freelance work, or it could manifest as some new opportunities for making money. The manifestation of money luck can take different forms, sometimes in ways that you least expect.

Money luck

Every person is born with a different astrological chart, so in the same way each person's money luck is different. But everyone has money luck. Make no mistake about this. Every person is born with the potential to become rich. The only difference from person to person is when this luck is going to ripen, and how big this luck is going to be. What feng shui can do is to speed up the ripening of your money luck. If you apply them correctly, water features are excellent for doing this.

Water features take many different forms. Usually a simple, decorative bowl with a small pump or an auspicious symbol is sufficient. This water feature shows the Fu dog, a protective symbol.

91 using the lucky corner methods to activate water

In this Tip and the next two, different methods are presented for energizing water. Each one has a different approach to water placement, which will attract the speedy ripening of your wealth luck.

The lucky corner of a room is the corner that is directly diagonal to the door. Place the water in the lucky corners of each room relative to the entrance. If this corner in your living room is free of encumbrances, with no toilets, store rooms, or staircases located behind here, then designing a water feature for this corner will be most auspicious.

You can also activate the lucky corner of your dining room if this corner can be clearly identified. The lucky corner method is derived from the form school method of feng shui. If it also corresponds to a lucky corner based on another method of computing the auspicious water corner, then you should definitely place a water feature here to boost your wealth prospects.

92 the period number for auspicious water

A second method used by feng shui experts to identify good corners for the placement of water features is based on the flying star period numbers method.

It has been calculated that for the current period of 7 and the coming period of 8, water will be auspicious when it is placed in the north, the east, the southeast, and the southwest. As the north is already the Water corner, activating it will be doubly auspicious. The east and southeast are Wood corners that will also benefit hugely from the placement of water (because Water produces

Wood in the Element Cycle.) So in these three compass direction corners of your living room you can place water features with confidence.

The southwest is the place of Earth and I would not normally be happy to place water here, but according to this method this corner is best for water between February 4th 2004 until February 4th 2024, i.e. in the forthcoming period of 8.

93 using flying star for water luck

This is the method that I feel most comfortable using. In fact, I have been repeatedly successful with this method in helping both myself and a great many other people gain higher incomes.

This simple method is good for those of you who do not yet know flying star, and who wish to capture the essence of wealth luck in your home using Water chi based on flying star.

You can refer to the table at the back of the book where I have summarized the most auspicious wealth corners for each of 16 different types of houses of this period of 7. If your home was built or renovated during the period of 7 (this is between February 4th 1984 and February 4th 2004) you can use this table to identify your wealth corner based on your main door's outward facing direction. Remember the principle of big chi and small chi, so this corner can apply to your whole house or to individual rooms. You must also note water taboos when activating water under this method (see Tip 95,) so never place water features in the bedroom.

94 waterfalls make millionaires

It is great fun thinking up all of the water enhancers and energizers that you can place in the auspicious water corners of your home. These can be waterfalls or aquariums.

But do not activate more than one corner of each room. Too much water can be excessively yin, and will drown you. Also, please note that the artificial water features shaped like long funnels with artificial fish swimming inside are not effective feng shui water features. For water objects to work there needs to be a body of water. So the water must be inside a container, which suggests some depth and volume. It is also necessary to see this body of water, only then will it be effective as a symbol of wealth creation. It is for this reason that fish aquariums and fish ponds work so well. Here there is a body of water that suggests that water has accumulated and is kept safe for the household. In my own home I also use decorative ceramic and porcelain containers to keep small goldfish in the wealth corner of my family dining room. These are about two to three feet in diameter and are placed at floor level. They are most effective and make extremely decorative features, especially when the water is lit.

Using water fountains

You can also activate a water feature with miniature water fountains that circulate water into the air and down again into a container. This causes a very yang process to get activated and is a very good way of bringing yang energy to water. I have seen this method used with great success, although personally I prefer aquariums and miniature ponds.

Water in the garden

Outside in the garden, you can create a waterfall in the wealth corner, making sure that the water is flowing towards the entrance to your home. This can potentially be a most powerful method, but it requires a big budget to create. I have seen this work extremely well for several of my business-men friends. They built waterfalls in their gardens and became multi-millionaires several times over. So from being moderately successful they have now become seriously wealthy, and they all swear by their waterfalls! If you have the land and the money, and you want to become really wealthy, use the chart on page 134 to identify the wealth corner of your land (based on the outward-facing direction of your house) and build your waterfall. Just make certain that the water falls down and flows towards your house, not away from it.

Man-made waterfalls are excellent feng shui, especially when cleverly designed to blend harmoniously with the garden space. It should not be too large, and then it will bring enormous wealth luck. Waterfalls can also be very small, designed specially for the indoor enhancement of space. Both work with equal potency. The best waterfalls have six levels of falls, as this signifies luck coming from heaven.

95

water taboos — where never to place water

It is important to observe water taboos diligently. Certain rooms and parts of the home should not be activated with water, otherwise they could well bring misfortune.

When water is placed incorrectly, different types of bad luck are manifested, but perhaps the worst is when serious problems arise between husband and wife. Marriages can break up and even sex scandals may occur.

Water in the bedroom

Firstly, never place water features (as described in Tip 95) in your bedrooms. The presence of even a small body of water in the bedroom will cause you to lose money and get cheated. How much money you lose will depend on your own luck, so it could be big or small. Water in the bedroom also causes the relationship between the husband and wife to cool and eventually die off, as the yin energy here gets afflicted causing relationships to become increasingly uncomfortable and unhappy.

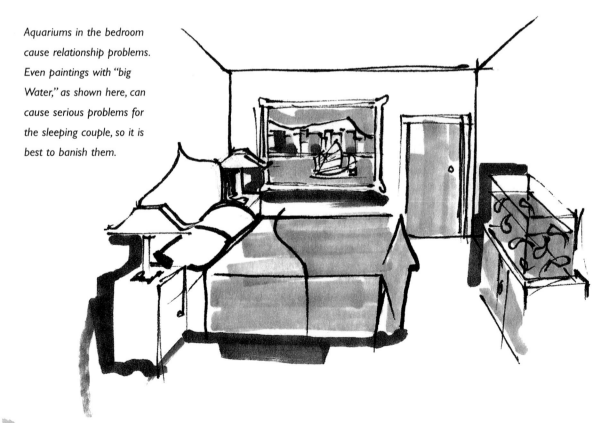

Aquariums in the bedroom cause relationship problems. Even paintings with "big Water," as shown here, can cause serious problems for the sleeping couple, so it is best to banish them.

Water on the right of your main entrance door causes problems in a marriage.

Water in bedrooms afflicts the Earth energy, thereby spoiling relationships. So do remove aquariums and small water fountains from your bedrooms. Ideally, do not even place a painting of the sea or of a lake in the bedroom. Glasses of water by the bedside do not count. A blue bedroom also does not count as water. It is the body of water that does harm, nothing else.

Water outside the front door

Secondly, never place water features on the right-hand side of your main entrance door as you look out of your door (whether inside or outside the house.) This position will cause the man of the house to develop a roving eye. Sometimes, this roving eye does not stop at harmless flirtations, but could cause tragic and scandalous consequences for the wife and family of the household. Water near the main door can bring wealth luck if those corners correspond to wealth corners, but it

is no use having wealth if it breaks up the family, or worse loses you your husband. The feng shui texts on this point stress that water on the right-hand side of the door causes romance and sex scandals, so wives and mothers should watch this particular taboo.

Water features under the stairs

Thirdly, you should refrain from placing any kind of water feature under the staircase. If yours is a staircase with some space below, do not think of installing a fountain or fishpond there. The water feature may look beautiful and nicely landscaped but it will adversely affect your children's wealth luck. At best, it might cause them to have difficulty finding jobs later on when they grow up. At worse, it can cause them to "lose out" in the inheritance stakes. The patriarch of the family will leave or die, or they will lose out in legal wrangling over family inheritance. Keep the empty space under the staircase as a store room, if you wish, but never place anything there that you know will suffer from being stepped over.

A water feature, such as the aquarium shown here, harms the luck of the family's children when placed under the staircase.

96 yin water absorbs bad chi from neighbors

When you activate water inside the home or around the garden you should note the difference between yin and yang water. One is good as a remedy, the other is an energizer.

Yin water is quiet and still. Its presence inside the home is as a remedy for excessive yang energy. It is also an excellent cure for some of the afflictions caused by deadly flying star afflictions. And indeed if you have bad neighbors, who are too loud or quarrelsome, you can simply place a large container of still water by the side of your home that is closest to them and let the water absorb all their negative energy. Yin water must be changed at least once a week otherwise it grows stale and can become harmful.

Yang water, on the other hand, is water that is said to be alive and bubbling. It is the kind of water that should be used to energize for wealth luck. Aquariums with live fish are considered yang water; ponds with carp or arrowana have yang water; tortoise ponds have yang water. So any kind of animal life inside the water will make it yang.

Bubbling water features

Another form of yang water is bubbling water created by air pumps. These are even better manifestations of yang chi, and in fact can be used to activate water whether or not you have fish living in your water. Yang water should also be kept clean with filtration systems and also simply by changing the water. Never let the water become stale or polluted. If you keep fish in your

Place a tub of water to contain loud noise from neighbors.

aquarium, you must invest in a filtration system that is in good working order. Nothing brings bad feng shui faster than chi that has become negative and dirty, and therefore afflicted.

Lily or lotus ponds

A third form of yang water is water features with plants growing in them. Therefore, water lily or lotus ponds are really good feng shui. When the plants bloom it signifies good fortune arising from negative or dire circumstances. So keeping lotus or water lilies is most auspicious if you have a pond in a good corner of your garden. Once you understand yang water you can differentiate between the way you use water – whether it is for energizing for good luck, or as a remedy to absorb excessive noise and stress from bad flying stars or neighbors.

97 water in wood sectors to attract growth

A final use of Water Element chi is to use it to enhance the Wood Element corners of your home. These are east and southeast corners of the house or of any room.

The east corner affects the luck of the eldest son of the family. To the Chinese the eldest son is the dynastic son whose fortunes are tied up with the family's descendants luck. Therefore, the east sector should be activated with good chi energy, which will cause the family's descendants luck to be secure and meaningful. Placing water in a Wood corner is very beneficial as Water produces Wood in the Element Cycle. Just remember, never go over the top. Doing too much is bad.

The southeast corner

This area affects the eldest daughter's luck. It also represents wealth under the Pa Kua method of feng shui analysis. Keeping the southeast corner of your home well energized will attract good chi into these special areas of your life. Water will also activate the growth energy of Wood.

Unless these corners also correspond to your wealth or lucky corners it is not necessary to activate with a body of water. All you need to do is just use the symbols of water to suggest the presence of water energy. For example, you could use water motifs, water patterns, or incorporate the blue or black or even purple into your color scheme. These are all wonderful symbols of water energy that will benefit these Wood sectors.

A picture of a harbor in the east benefits sons; in the southeast, daughters benefit.

Water symbolism

Paintings of water scenery and photographs showing water are also beneficial in these Wood corners of the home or of the living room. So place these to fine-tune your interior decoration ideas. You will find that if you systematically apply these feng shui fine points to your home decor, the energy will become very balanced and auspicious. You will find yourself looking forward to coming home each day and your house will feel truly welcoming. When you feel this, you will agree with me when I say that the results can truly be quite magical.

98 boosting wood corners with plants and flowers

Wood Element chi symbolizes growth, expansion, and new beginnings. Wood relates to the east and the southeast. Wood chi brings material success that comes from growth and upward mobility.

Like the branches of a tree, good luck grows ever outwards and upwards. Wood is the only Element that has life and the innate ability to expand. Its nature and essence are therefore different from the other four Elements. Wood energy also confers descendants' luck on families, and is beneficial to the sons of the family.

Auspicious plants in the east

Good feng shui always considers luck beyond the first generation, and in fact the feng shui masters of olden days always saw feng shui in terms of several generations. So it is an excellent idea to fill the eastern part of the home with beautiful plants and flowers. There are also special auspicious flowers which the Chinese favor above others. The yellow chrysanthemum is considered most auspicious, and wealthy Chinese homes always display these flowers whenever they are in season. Other auspicious flowers are white magnolias, peonies of all shades and hues, the beautiful plum blossom, and the orchid. Always follow feng shui guidelines about avoiding plants that are prickly or flowers with thorns – especially hidden thorns, which are never considered good.

Healthy growing plants are also most auspicious in the growth sectors of the home. If you do not have real plants, or find them hard to grow, the fake plants or trees that come with silk leaves are most suitable. Just avoid having dead plants or dried flowers in the vibrant growth sector – nothing kills the chi here faster! So when you display fresh flowers make sure you throw them out the moment they start to rot. The rotting process immediately creates harmful yin chi.

Plants should look healthy and vibrant. Fake flowers can bring good chi, but dried flowers are never recommended. The auspicious magnolia, orchid, and chrysanthemum.

Magnolia

Orchid

Chrysanthemum

99

flowers for luck throughout the year

Traditionally, some Chinese families display four-season flowers in the form of paintings or porcelain and other decorative objects.

The presence of these flowers indicates good luck throughout the year. The Chinese know that feng shui has a time dimension and that through the course of the year as the months change so too does the intangible chi that pervades the space. So there will always be symbols in the home that attempt to reduce the effects of bad and afflicted stars.

Symbols in the east and southeast

One more important thing to have in the east and southeast, using either the real thing or pictorially, are what the Chinese refer to as the three friends in winter. These are the branch of the pine tree, which signifies longevity; the plum blossom, which has the ability to blossom in adversity; and the bamboo, which symbolizes the wisdom to accommodate the prevailing winds of circumstance and spring back with effortless resilience when times get better. When they are present in the home, these three friends of winter will ensure that the family always survives any change in their fortunes.

Good feng shui

When you have this, you will not even know you are living through hard times until after it is all over and you look back and realize you have just

The three friends in winter symbolize strength in adversity: the pine, plum blossom, and bamboo.

The bamboo represents resilience

The plumb blossom symbolizes strength

The pine signifies longevity

come though a bad period. Great feng shui shields you from feeling the evil brunt of hard times, enabling you to live through them with equanimity and even some humor.

100 wood fuels fire for recognition luck

Wood energy brings wonderful fuel to the southern sectors of any home. Here it takes on a different complexion, and it is old rather than young wood that provides sustenance for the Fire energy.

In the cycle of Elements, it is the Element that produces another Element that is regarded as having the ability to create the luck that is needed for growth and expansion. So if you want your good name to spread far and wide and need the acceptance of a wider and ever growing circle of supporters, then remember to boost or fuel the Fire of the south.

You can create Wood energy in the south by introducing wood panelling here, or have a wooden floor fitted rather than laying carpets or stone tiles.

101 metal chi is harmful in wood sectors

Metal has the power to destroy growth. In the Wood sectors metal cuts and strikes with a chilling efficiency that will shake you quite badly.

Never, ever display swords and guns on the east wings of your home. Only use Metal energy in the east if it is very badly afflicted and the Wood energy is spoiled because of several toilets located there, or when the intangible annual stars here are the harmful stars.

To overcome afflicted Wood energy, do not use a windchime. Instead, it is better to use a small curved metal knife that you can hang on the wall. Hide it away, if you like, if a toilet is located here.

So make sure your bells and windchimes are never hung here unless they are made of bamboo or crystal. Yes, there are bamboo chimes and crystal bells that possess the attributes of these symbols but with different Element chi attached to them. Bamboo chimes activate Wood chi but these do not possess anywhere near the same power as Metal windchimes. Crystal bells, on the other hand, are excellent purveyors of chi as crystal is such a powerful purveyor of Earth energy.

102

powerful metal energy

Metal chi brings the luck of patrons and relates to children. The essence of Metal is that it is unbending, yet it is also very potent, especially when attracting luck for the family patriarch.

Metal is the Element of the west and north-west. It symbolizes heaven power and leadership. It is associated with gold, and its energy is dense and inward flowing. If you successfully tap auspicious Metal chi, you will create the chi that brings power and great influence to the household.

Activating metal energy

The best way to stimulate Metal energy is to hang Metal windchimes or bells in the west and north-west corners of your home. These two symbolic objects are very powerful. They do not merely bring the presence of Metal into your corners, they also have the potential to create the sound of Metal. When you hang windchimes, make sure they are all-metal rather than metal and wood. Six rods signify the Big Metal chi of the northwest.

Special windchimes

Also, avoid hanging windchimes with different mobiles hanging from them. The best windchimes to hang are all-metal windchimes, as these symbolize the bare attributes associated metal. A "wu lo" on top acts as a protective health symbol which can keep illness at bay. It also symbolizes spiritual blessings and the emblem of the God of longevity.

Hanging a pagoda windchime in the west sector benefits the family's children, especially those embarking on scholarly pursuits connected with their future careers. Hanging a windchime in the northwest benefits the family patriarch. It is a good idea to place a fan to stimulate the chimes to sound, or place them in a breezy part of the room near windows. The sound of metal not only activates good luck; it can dissolve any bad energy brought by intangible flying stars. So even without you knowing, the windchimes are protecting you from illness and loss caused by bad flying stars. This is due mainly to the power of Metal in countering afflicted Earth energy.

Sitting under windchimes

There is only thing to remember about windchimes and that is that you should never sit under them. No matter how auspicious a symbol is, you should never have it above your head. In any case, Metal above the head always suggests a weapon poised to strike. This is because in the old days swords, knives, and weapons of aggression were all associated with the Metal Element.

103 earth energy cuts both ways

Earth is the grounding energy, and it manifests the core of feng shui. Tapping Earth luck brings harmony and family happiness, usually associated with the matriarch.

It also encourages romantic happiness and signifies the successful acquisition of knowledge. Earth dominates the southwest, the northeast, and the center grid of any home. If you divide your home into the Lo Shu grid (see Tip 12) you will discover that the Earth sectors form a diagonal across the grid. This demonstrates the all-pervasive force of mother Earth energy. In fact, some experts tell me that when the chi of your home has healthy Earth energy, which is not afflicted, the feng shui of that home is said to be exceptionally good.

Earth houses

Homes that face either southwest or northeast are said to be Earth chi houses. This is the northeast/southwest axis, which emphasizes the power of the matriarch. Such homes manifest great good fortune for the women of the household but more than that, they possess exceptional good family and relationship luck.

Boosting Earth chi

The best way to activate Earth chi is to fill your home with crystal, porcelain, ceramics, marble, or terrazzo floors and lots of bright lights. Marble and granite are strong; Earth making the home very grounded, and the chi very stable. Such houses enjoy excellent stability of good fortune.

Bad afflictions

But Earth energy cuts both ways and during the years when the southwest and northeast sectors of any home are afflicted by the deadly five yellow, which is itself seriously afflicted Earth energy, then that is when Earth chi turns to bad energy. It can bring loss, illness, and serious accidents. During the years when this affliction takes place, make sure that you hang metal windchimes in the affected areas as they have the power to exhaust the bad Earth energy.

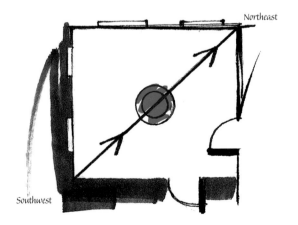

Of the three Earth corners, the southwest brings relationships, the northeast brings wisdom, and the center brings family luck.

104

harness earth chi to benefit the matriarch

When you harness Earth chi in any home the mother, as well as all the women of the household, will benefit, but maternal energy usually brings luck to the whole family.

The corner that signifies the mother is the southwest, so this is the corner that must be protected if you want to guard the mother's luck. Remember that the trigram here is K'un which also has the attributes of the mare.

Boosting mother energy

Place the image of a mare here and the mother energy becomes quite awesome. Another way to activate the matriarchal energy is to hang a painting of an empress in the front of the home, because if you see an auspicious painting of an authoritative, powerful woman as you enter, it will surely empower the mother in the household. I have to confess that in my own home I have a stunning painting of the Lady of the Nine Heavens. She is shown seated like an empress, a little plump, but very prosperous looking indeed. And she is pointing to a Luo Pan (Chinese feng shui compass) as if explaining its meaning. I commissioned this painting from an artist in China, and ever since it has taken center stage in my home, I have personally felt very empowered. To me the Lady of the Nine Heavens is very significant for it is she who first brought down the Luo Pan and handed it to the yellow emperor. If you know the legend of this lady, you will understand why I consider it is she who is the real founder of compass formula feng shui, and why she holds such a special place in my heart.

Good matriarchal energy

Families where the matriarchal energy is well energized and protected tend to stay together. Also, because the family unit features so strongly as criteria for judging good fortune, this aspect of feng shui practice receives a great deal of attention. If you are female and have Kua numbers 5 or 8 (see Tip 107) you will benefit twice over if you energize the southwest corner of your home. Also, those of you with Kua number 8 will benefit hugely and enjoy enormous good luck during the coming period of 8, which starts February 4th 2004 and lasts 20 years.

Always use a compass correctly when locating the southwest for the matriarch, and for any other cardinal or secondary direction. Hold your compass flat on your hand and stand square. Directions in feng shui should always be as accurate as possible.

105

the deadly "five yellow" – an afflicted earth star

Earth energy turns hostile when hit by invisible flying stars, which create havoc even in a home with the best feng shui. It is extremely useful to know about the five yellow.

Even if you are unfamiliar with flying star feng shui it is important for you to know that there is a time dimension in feng shui practice. Time stars can cause havoc, but you can protect yourself against the malevolent effects of these intangible and invisible "stars."

The negativity of the five yellow

One of the most harmful of these stars is the star number 5, called the five yellow. The chi essence of this star is Earth, but it is afflicted Earth and whenever it appears in sectors of your home that house the main door or your bedroom, you will feel its full negative impact. In some years this five yellow is more harmful than others, and the severity of its impact is based on which sector it flies into. So in 1999 when it flew into the south its effect was extremely potent for those hurt by it. This was because the south is the Fire Element and Fire enhances Earth in the Element Cycle. In 2000 the five yellow was in the north where it did less damage, as Water overcomes Earth.

Movements of the flying yellow

In 2001 it will fly into the southwest where it will create massive bad luck for all homes that face either southwest or northeast. So if your home faces either of these directions, please hang a six-rod windchime both at the entrance as well as at the back of the house. This is because the southwest and northeast are strong Earth sectors that enhance the strength of the five yellow. So whether your house is facing or sitting in the southwest (note that when your home faces northeast, you are said to be sitting in the southwest) you will be affected by the five yellow and will need to take precautions. If your bedroom is in the southwest, you should also hang a windchime there, or ideally, move to another room.

In 2002 and 2003 the five yellow flies to the east and southeast respectively, and in these two sectors, it loses some of its strength to hurt, because in these Wood sectors Earth loses strength immediately as Wood conquers Earth in the Element Cycle. Do not hang a windchime here as it is not necessary, and also because the Metal chi of the windchime harms the inherent Wood chi.

In later years

In 2004 the five yellow flies to the center of the house and here again it creates massive harm. This is because this area also belongs to the Earth energy. In 2005 it flies to the northwest, where it again loses strength as the Big Metal of the northwest overcomes and exhausts its energy.

106

becoming familiar with the five elements

By now you will have a very good idea of how Element energy works inside and outside your home. Here are a few tips to help you remember how to use the Elements.

Firstly, note that when we assign Elements to the eight compass directions we are using the Yang Pa Kua, also known as the later heaven arrangement of trigrams around the eight sides.

Secondly, the Elements are assigned according to the trigrams. So Ch'ien is always Metal and K'un is always Earth. The trigram Kan is always Water and Li is always Fire. So when you use the Later Heaven Pa Kua you will see that since Ch'ien is placed in the northwest, then that is where Metal is, and as K'un is southwest that is the place of Earth, and so forth. In learning this, you will find that feng shui will become much easier to understand. But more importantly, it will prepare you for the more complex interpretations of the advanced compass school formulations. Remember that Elements feature in all the interpretations and applications of feng shui

Elements and numbers

Thirdly, Elements are also connected to numbers. Each number from 1 to 9 is associated with one of the Five Elements. And again this is based on the attributes of the Later Heaven Pa Kua. So 1 is Water; 2, 5, and 8 are Earth; 3 and 4 are Wood; 6 and 7 are Metal; and 9 is Fire. Again learn these associations. There are only five Elements and they are easy to learn.

Element colors and shapes

Fourthly, the Elements are associated with colors, with a yin and yang aspect. Some colors are more yin than yang, but their Element associations are more potent. So note that red is Fire, blue and black are Water, green and brown are Wood, beige and yellow are Earth, and white and gold are Metal.

Fifthly, even shapes have Element connotations. Wood is rectangular, Fire is triangular, Earth is square, Metal is round, and Water is wavy.

There are a great deal more Element associations – they relate to the seasons of the year, to musical notes, and so on. It is not necessary to know all the associations, but knowing the basics will enable you to be empowered in your feng shui practice and it will also allow you to fine-tune your applications. So if you wish to strengthen the use of Metal in the northwest, you can put six windchimes instead of a single windchime. Why? Because the northwest is associated with 6 and metal links to 6. If you want to put a tortoise in the north to activate the Water there, you will know that a single tortoise will be most powerful. This is because 1 is the number of the north and Water.

Once you are thoroughly familiar with the Elements and how their chi essence works, you are ready to move on to the next level of practice.

summary of auspicious wealth and relationship sectors

The following applies only to houses or buildings completed or renovated from February 4th 1984 to February 4th 2004 (period of 7.) Check the orientation of your main door and then determine the most auspicious wealth and relationship sector in your home. (This table is based on flying star water and mountain stars 8.)

ORIENTATION OF BUILDING OR DIRECTION OF MAIN DOOR	THE EXACT BEARING IN DEGREES READ FROM THE COMPASS	MOST AUSPICIOUS RELATIONSHIP SECTOR	MOST AUSPICIOUS WEALTH SECTOR
SOUTH 1	157.5 TO 172.5	NORTH	NORTHEAST
SOUTH 2	172.5 TO 187.5	SOUTH	SOUTHWEST
SOUTH 3	187.5 TO 202.5	SOUTH	SOUTHWEST
SOUTHWEST 1	**202.5 TO 217.5**	**EAST**	**NORTH**
SOUTHWEST 2	**217.5 TO 232.5**	**WEST**	**SOUTH**
SOUTHWEST 3	**232.5 to 247.5**	**WEST**	**SOUTH**
WEST 1	247.5 TO 262.5	NORTHEAST	SOUTHEAST
WEST 2	262.5 TO 277.5	SOUTHWEST	NORTHWEST
WEST 3	277.5 TO 292.5	SOUTHWEST	NORTHWEST
NORTHWEST 1	**292.5 TO 307.5**	**SOUTH**	**WEST**
NORTHWEST 2	**307.5 TO 322.5**	**NORTH**	**EAST**
NORTHWEST 3	**322.5 TO 337.5**	**NORTH**	**EAST**
NORTH 1	337.5 TO 352.5	NORTHEAST	NORTH
NORTH 2	352.5 TO 007.5	SOUTHWEST	SOUTH
NORTH 3	007.5 TO 022.5	SOUTHWEST	SOUTH
NORTHEAST 1	**022.5 TO 037.5**	**NORTH**	**EAST**
NORTHEAST 2	**037.5 TO 052.5**	**SOUTH**	**WEST**
NORTHEAST 3	**052.5 TO 067.5**	**SOUTH**	**WEST**
EAST 1	067.5 TO 082.5	SOUTHEAST	NORTHEAST
EAST 2	082.5 TO 097.5	NORTHWEST	SOUTHWEST
EAST 3	097.5 TO 112.5	NORTHWEST	SOUTHWEST
SOUTHEAST 1	**112.5 TO 127.5**	**CENTER**	**EAST**
SOUTHEAST 2	**127.5 TO 142.5**	**CENTER**	**WEST**
SOUTHEAST 3	**142.5 TO 157.5**	**CENTER**	**WEST**

4

personalizing

feng shui

practice with

eight mansions

107 kua numbers and eight mansions feng shui

The Eight Mansions method of feng shui is a compass formula which categorizes people into East and West groups. From this arises many powerful feng shui applications.

I call this the Pa Kua, Lo Shu formula, simply because the application of this formula is based on the Yang Pa Kua and Lo Shu Square.

The Eight Mansions formula derives from classical Chinese texts on determining auspicious directions and locations for people, which are determined by their birth dates and gender. The formula is therefore a personalized approach to the practice of feng shui. It is easy to apply, and there are myriad ways of using it.

How to find your Kua number

- Start using this formula by determining your personal auspicious and inauspicious directions. To do this, you will need to work out your personal Kua number. To calculate your Kua number you need your lunar year of birth and your gender. The lunar year of birth is determined by the date of your birth. If you were born between 1 January and 20 February, you need to check the date on which the lunar New Year happened in your year of birth. If you were born before the New Year, subtract one year from your year of birth before calculating your Kua number, so if you were born on 19 January 1966, count your birth year as 1965.

- Check against the Table of lunar years on page 215 at the back of this book, and then use the calculation given here to find your personal Kua number.

For men:

- Take your lunar year of birth, add together the last two digits, reduce it to a single number, then subtract this from 10 to get your Kua number.
- Example 1: Year of birth 1964 – 6+4=10 and 1+0=1, 10-1= 9. The Kua number is 9.
- Example 2: Year of birth 1984 – 8+4=12 and 1+2=3, 10-3 = 7 so the Kua is 7.
- Note: for boys born after 2000, subtract from 9 instead of 10.

For women:

- Take the lunar year of birth and add together the last two digits, reduce to a single number, and then add 5. If the result is more than 10 reduce to a single digit. The result is your Kua number.
- Example 1: Year of birth 1945 – 4+5=9 then 9+5=14, 1+4=5 so the Kua is 5.
- Example 2: Year of birth 1982 – 8+2=10 and 1+0=1, 1+5=6 so the Kua is 6.

108 your kua number is a powerful feng shui tool

With your Kua number, you are armed with a powerful tool; it enables you to align all your personal orientations to synchronize with your living space.

This is because the Kua number gives you your four auspicious directions and your four inauspicious directions. By knowing your good and bad orientations, you can use them in different ways to improve your feng shui.

East or West group?

By your Kua number alone, you will know if you belong to the East or West group directions. You will also discover:

- Your four auspicious directions and your four inauspicious directions.

- The best direction to use for study, meditation, and personal development, and the best one to use at work to enhance your success potential.

- The best direction to improve your health and get well after an illness.

- The best direction to use to improve your relationships luck.

- Which part of your home and which directions are bad for you.

- Which corner of the house is good for you, and which will bring you the best luck.

In fact, the Eight Mansions method of feng shui is so broad-based and comprehensive that many experts who use it acknowledge that practicing this one method alone is sufficient to enjoy great feng shui.

Using your best directions

The stunning thing about this Kua method is that it is also the easiest to use. Even a homeless tramp, sleeping with his head pointed to his best direction on the street, will find his luck changing for the better.

The poor student facing his best direction while he works, and sleeping with his head oriented to his personal growth direction, could well win him – or herself – a much needed scholarship.

If you write out a job application while facing your best direction, your chances of getting employment increase enormously.

If you negotiate any kind of deal while facing your best direction, you put yourself in a good feng shui position immediately. The business person who knows how to sit to tap his directions will have the edge over the business person who does not know them!

I have used this formula myself for over 25 years with the most amazing success. Despite how easy it is to use, it has never failed me.

109

kua numbers reveal lucky/unlucky directions

Eight Mansions feng shui explains that everyone is either an East- or a West-group person. Generally, people of the same group tend to be more compatible.

East-group people get along better with other East-group people and the same is true of West-group people. Whether you are an East-group or West-group person depends on your Kua number.

East-group people have the Kua numbers 1, 3, 4, and 9 and their four auspicious directions are north, south, southeast, and east. These are the east group directions and any one of these directions will bring good luck to people in this group.

The good and bad directions

West-group people have the Kua numbers 5, 2, 6, 7, and 8 and for this group the four auspicious directions are west, southwest, northwest, and northeast. If you are a west-group person, any one of these directions will bring you good fortune and good luck.

Now please also take note that East-group directions are inauspicious for West-group people and vice versa. You should commit your Kua number and your auspicious directions to memory so that you will always know your lucky and unlucky directions in any situation. Carry a compass with you always and you can practice this simple feng shui technique wherever you are.

Just knowing if you are East- or West-group allows you to ensure you never face or sleep with your head pointed to an unlucky direction ever again in your life. And as long as you live in a state of awareness of the energy flow in the environment, your chi will always blend harmoniously with that of your space. This implies that you will always make the effort to orientate your sitting and sleeping direction in accordance with your group of lucky directions. Moreover, when you have grown familiar with your directions and have made this awareness a part of your daily habits, you will continually discover fresh uses for the formula. For instance, I always make sure I face my success direction when I am negotiating an important contract, when I am making an important phone call, or when I am giving a lecture or a presentation. Over the years, I like to think of this state of awareness of my living space as one of my success habits. You can do the same. Just remember not to let ease of practice fool you into thinking any less of the formula.

110

there are four types of good luck

Eight Mansions feng shui describes four types of good luck. From your four auspicious directions, you will see that they each can be fine-tuned to bring in four different types of good fortune.

How these are determined is again based on your Kua number. So now when you tap into these good luck directions you will benefit from the special chi attached to them. First determine what kind of luck you want to focus on, and then find out which direction applies to you based on your Kua number, using the table shown below.

You will discover that there is a kind of hierarchy to the four good directions, and therefore types of luck, that belong to either the East or West group of directions. So it is important to be clear about your priorities before choosing the direction you want to activate.

- Wealth and success luck comes from your Sheng Chi direction.

- Health and longevity luck is brought by your Tien Yi direction.

- Love, marriage, and family luck are brought by your Nien Yen direction.

- Growth, personal development, and advancement luck is brought by your Fu Wei direction.

Your different good luck directions according to your Kua number

KUA NUMBER	SHENG CHI	TIEN YI	NIEN YEN	FU WEI
	Wealth	**Health**	**Love**	**Growth**
I	Southeast	East	South	North
2	Northeast	West	Northwest	Southwest
3	South	North	Southeast	East
4	North	South	East	Southeast
5 (men)	Northeast	West	Northwest	Southwest
5 (women)	Southwest	Northwest	West	Northeast
6	West	Northeast	Southwest	Northwest
7	Northwest	Southwest	Northeast	West
8	Southwest	Northwest	West	Northeast
9	East	Southeast	North	South

111 there are four types of bad luck

Eight Mansions feng shui also differentiates between four types of bad luck. The direction that brings each of these misfortunes is again unique to each Kua number.

So if you want to avoid bad luck, you should determine your four bad luck directions and simply never face them when you work or when discussing important matters. You should also try not to sleep with your head pointing towards these harmful directions. So note that:

- Mild bad luck, the kind that causes you to have accidents, small losses, and headaches – annoying rather than serious things – is brought from your Ho Hai direction.

- The bad luck of "five ghosts," for example, troublemakers politicking against you or people who want to harm you. This bad luck is brought from your Wu Kwei direction.

- The bad luck of six killings – the six types of misfortunes, which in some cases can be serious. This is brought from your Lui Shar direction.

- The serious bad luck of total loss is brought from your Chueh Ming direction. This is the worst kind of misfortune and often suggests bankruptcy and death. When your astrological period is bad and you sit or sleep tapping this direction, Chueh Ming can bring a disaster.

Your different bad luck directions according to your Kua number

KUA NUMBER	HO HAI Mishaps	WU KWEI Five ghosts	LUI SHAR Six killings	CHUEH MING Total loss
1	West	Northeast	Northwest	Southwest
2	East	Southeast	South	North
3	Southwest	Northwest	Northeast	West
4	Northwest	Southwest	West	Northeast
5 (men)	East	Southeast	South	North
5 (women)	South	North	East	Southeast
6	Southeast	East	North	South
7	North	South	Southeast	East
8	South	North	East	Southeast
9	Northeast	West	Southwest	Northwest

116

windows can take the place of doors

If you do not have a door that faces one of your four excellent Kua directions, see if you can activate an auspicious window instead.

Open it as often as possible, and look out of this window often so that symbolically you receive the chi that comes from that direction. If the view is good the luck is further enhanced. For example, if there is a view of water or of a river which is flowing past the window, then this will make up for the fact that you cannot tap one of your important directions from the main door.

Other lucky windows

You can have more than one lucky window. In fact if you can find lucky windows that face all four of your good directions, it is a good idea to energize all four windows by opening them as much as you can. Once again you can activate windows according to where they are located in terms of the compass orientation of your home. Also, once you know the direction that the good chi is coming from through the window, it is a good idea to place an energizer near it to draw in the good chi.

You can also make a big feature of an auspicious window and activate the luck there by placing such fortuitous decorative objects as a sailing ship laden with ingots; crystals; and healthy, round-leaved plants. However, dirty, cracked glass, or peeling paintwork is bad feng shui so you must repair and clean the window ledges before you activate this area, otherwise all you will do is magnify the inauspicious energy, creating bad situations for yourself.

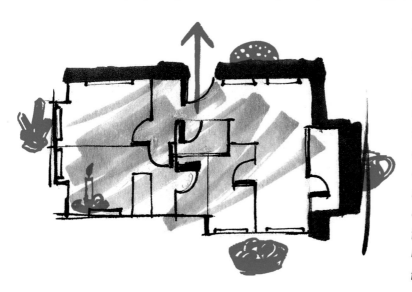

Windows that face north: place a sponge near the window to draw in Water energy. Windows that face south: put some wood near it to attract in Fire energy. Windows that face east or southeast: position a jug of water to attract Wood energy. Windows that face west or northwest: place some crystals to attract Metal energy. Windows that face northeast or southwest: put a lighted candle (but only when you are present) to attract in Earth energy.

117 solid doors are better than sliding or glass doors

All the important doors of your home should be solid. These include the main door as well as the doors that lead into your bedrooms. This defines your living space in a more auspicious way.

Sliding doors and doors made of glass can be used for your secondary doors. Solid doors indicate proper protection for the home and symbolically keep out bad chi. When the main door is weak it also means that your home is not safe against intruders and bad chi can enter.

Another feng shui point about main doors is that ideally they should be the largest door into the home. When the main door is smaller than other doors in the home it implies that the family living there will get bullied and taken advantage of by others.

Secondary doors

A third item about doors to consider is if there are any secondary entrance doors that support your main door. These are good feng shui, so if you do have them your feng shui has been considerably enhanced. Note the following:

- If your main door is located in the north, then a secondary door in the west or northwest will be good for the home.

- If the main door is located in the southern part of the home, then a secondary door in the east or southeast will be beneficial for the home. These features will be especially good for East-group people with Kua numbers 1, 3, 4, and 9.

- If your main door is located in the southwest or northeast corner of your home, then a secondary door in the southern sector will be good for the home.

- If the main door is located in the west or northwest part of the home, then a secondary door in the southwest or northeast will be good for the home. These features will be especially good for West-group people with Kua numbers 2, 5, 6, 7, and 8.

118 boosting luck with windows

Windows that open outwards are always luckier than windows that slide up and down. This is because when the windows open outwards they are actually inviting in luck.

Having said this, however, many people have windows that slide up and down. To enhance the luck of such windows, it is a good idea to frame the window with a darker colored paint. Let the chi outside be made aware that there is an opening through which it can enter the home. It is also a good idea to keep the window open as much as possible.

119 sleeping for success

Your sleeping direction is a vital part of personal feng shui. With the correct direction of sleep, you get hours of good fortune accumulating.

The best way to benefit from good feng shui when you sleep is to make sure that the crown of your head is tapping your success chi. So your head must be pointing towards your Sheng Chi direction. If this is not possible, make sure it is pointing to at least one of your four good directions while you are sleeping.

Sleeping in your best direction harnesses success luck. This is fundamental in bedroom feng shui so, wherever possible, orientate your bed so that you sleep in a direction that brings you good fortune.

KUA NUMBER	BEST SLEEPING DIRECTION
1	Southeast
2	Northeast
3	South
4	North
5 (Male)	Northeast
5 (Female)	Southwest
6	West
7	Northwest
8	Southwest
9	East

120 activating your "nien yen" for love

A powerful application of Eight Mansions is to use it to keep your love life radiant and happy. For this, activate your Nien Yen, which in Chinese means "longevity with rich descendants."

To the Chinese, love luck means family luck as well as romance. By sleeping with your head pointed towards your Nien Yen, or love direction, you will enhance all your existing family relationships and bring them into harmony. If you are single, it can help activate love luck to find you a new partner.

Good bedroom feng shui

Of course, you need to check that nothing is disrupting your bedroom feng shui or this powerful formula will be weakened. Water features, mirrors facing the bed, and poison arrows are all traditional culprits in this area and must be eliminated if you are to create the correct environment that nurtures restful sleep and positive luck. In nature, the bedroom should be very yin, or female, so active, yang energy represented by mirrors, for example, often causes an imbalance of energies that will dilute your attempts to harness your Nien Yen. Always assess your rooms for negative elements before you activate your personal feng shui.

Here I have summarized your best sleeping direction for love according to Kua numbers.

Mandarin ducks are powerful love enhancers.

Where to sleep for love

KUA NUMBER	BEST SLEEPING DIRECTION
1	South
2	Northwest
3	Southeast
4	East
5 (Male)	Northwest
5 (Female)	West
6	Southwest
7	Northeast
8	West
9	North

121 space constraints in sleeping directions

Sleeping in auspicious directions can often be difficult to get right, especially when you have space constraints. This is mainly because you need to follow general bedroom guidelines as well.

It is important to remember what to avoid in your bedroom before you tap into your auspicious sleeping direction. Here are the important pointers to follow:

- Never sleep with the bedroom door behind you or so that it cuts into the side of your bed.

- Also, never place the bed between two doors, such as the bedroom door and the door to an ensuite bathroom.

- Place cures where there are protruding corners. Hang windchimes over them to dispel the cutting energy, or shar chi that they create.

- Move the bed so it does not lie beneath an overhead beam as this can cause headaches and ill health. If the beam is positioned down the length of the bed, this creates a symbolic division between sleeping partners and must also be avoided. Hang a fabric canopy to create a false ceiling or, better still, move the bed out of the way.

- Do not have any mirrors in the bedroom. Those that reflect the bed are especially harmful. This is because the Chinese believe that seeing yourself reflected in a mirror disturbs the spirit, and this disturbance is bounced right back to you, causing bad chi and disharmony.

- Water in the bedroom is always bad feng shui. It is too

powerful an activator to be in this yin room. A glass of water at the bedside is acceptable; aquariums and other water features, even paintings of water, are not.

Finding an auspicious direction

When you move your bed to sleep in an auspicious direction, you may find that this creates serious feng shui problems that did not exist before. If the problems created are too great, always follow the general guidelines detailed first – it is much better to get these right than sacrifice all your good bedroom feng shui in order to sleep in your best direction.

If tapping your best direction means sleeping beneath a beam, it is best to move the bed.

122

when husband and wife are in different groups

A major difficulty encountered by many people when they try to practice Eight Mansions feng shui is when the husband and wife belong to different groups.

When one partner belongs to the West group and the other belongs to the East group, then what is good for one is hurtful for the other. Sometimes the Kua numbers are also such that the best direction for one is the killing direction for the other. There are several ways you can solve this problem. Consider the following solutions and see if you can implement any one of them in your particular situation.

Different entrances

Have two doors, one for him and one for her. This is the way I solved my own situation and it has worked well for my husband and I for the past 20 years. We also have our own sleeping direction by having two beds instead of one. And I use two rice cookers, one for him and one for me. This ensures that we can both tap our respective best directions. For western readers, have two microwaves or toasters: one for the husband and one for the wife, so that you can both eat from food cooked from two sets of chi. This is the easiest way of ensuring good food feng shui for you both.

Direction of the main door

For the main door, follow the husband's best direction. The Chinese feng shui masters reveal their subconscious chauvinism and bias towards the patriarch and indeed, in old China, women were regarded as being less important than the men and hence it was the man's best direction that would be the basis for arranging the feng shui of homes.

With all the other directions – sleeping, eating, and working – let these be based according to the individual Kua numbers.

123 negotiate for success with kua directions

You can use your auspicious directions in business negotiations, so that you harness good fortune and boost your wealth and career luck. Remember to carry a compass with you at all times.

You can do this by sitting so that you face your best direction or, if this is not possible, facing one of your other three good directions according to your Kua number (see the chart in Tip 107.) When you face your lucky directions, you will find that you feel more confident when negotiating with people, particularly if the person with whom you are negotiating is sitting in one of his or her bad directions. It is for this reason that as a business strategy you should always carry a pocket compass with you, and always make small talk with your associate so that you have the opportunity to find out his age, and thereby his year of birth. From there it is no problem to work out his or her Kua number in your head and identify the direction that would put him or her at a disadvantage.

Meetings away from the office

When the venue for your meeting is unfamiliar make sure that you get your orientation as soon as possible. You can also implement some of the guidelines of form school feng shui regarding the sitting taboos to avoid, such as not sitting facing a toilet or under a beam or where you will be hit by shar chi from a protruding corner. Many of these techniques are instinctive, but it is worth memorizing them so they are at the forefront of

your mind before you start negotiating. Practicing these rituals will make you feel more physically and mentally secure.

Where to sit during negotiations

• Sit furthest away from the door.

• Sit with a solid wall behind you for support.

• Don't sit anywhere where your feet point at the door, as this is considered a bad position.

• Never sit with your back to the door as you will worry about people coming up behind you.

• Avoid sitting anywhere near sharp corners, so if you have a choice use a round meeting table rather than a rectangular one.

Note good and bad sitting directions in the boardroom. Furthest away from the door is best.

124

sitting right to attract success

If you want success at work, then sit at your desk so you face your Sheng Chi, or best direction. When directions are flipped, it sets off a never-ending chain reaction.

This is the direction that also brings wealth and prosperity and tapping it when you are negotiating an important agreement, talking to your boss, or attending a crucial meeting will ensure success for you.

Important interviews or examinations

If you are taking an important examination, or attending an interview for a scholarship or a job that you want, you should try to tap some feng shui luck by sitting in your Fu Wei direction. This direction activates the luck of personal enhancement and development.

If you wish to activate the luck of love, then you should sit facing your Nien Yen (romance) direction. If health and longevity are your major concerns, sit facing your Tien Yi direction, which is also your direction of good health.

Buying the right compass

In using the directions for any of the purposes mentioned, buy a good western-style compass. Just remember that western compasses conventionally position the direction north at the top of the compass, while feng shui books such as this one usually illustrate compasses with north at the bottom. Readers should not let this confuse them, because the north or south or any direction mentioned in my books and in most feng shui books refers to the same north and south that is indicated on any compass, be it western or Chinese – there is no difference.

Living in the southern hemisphere

Another major point I wish to stress is that for those living in the southern hemisphere there is no necessity to "flip" the directions. I am perfectly aware that the equator, which is the source of global warmth, lies to the north for those in the southern hemisphere. I am also aware that the winds from the north bring warmth, and that this is therefore different from the Northern hemisphere. However, I want to stress that feng shui is really about more than warmth and cold. All sorts of factors are taken account of in feng shui formulas. Advanced feng shui speaks of different "plates" that place the north in different positions. So there are Man plates, Earth plates, and Heaven plates in traditional feng shui compasses. The differences in the directions of these plates can vary as much as fifteen degrees. So please do not flip the directions for the southern hemisphere as you will get all your feng shui wrong.

125

traveling from your auspicious directions

You can use feng shui in all areas of your life. When traveling, plan your feng shui so that your itinerary and route brings luck.

This should be closely adhered to if you are thinking of relocating, as this determines whether you are bringing good luck with you or not when you travel or relocate.

Using your best direction

The correct feng shui analysis is to travel from your best direction. Note this means you look at where you are traveling from rather than where you are traveling to. It is seldom easy to change one's route of travel, nor is it possible to easily change the direction of the destination. So if you

Take the starting place as your point of reference when calculating good and bad directions for travel.

need to travel from London to Bristol the direction of travel is set and there is nothing you can do about it. Similarly, if you have to travel from London to Boston you are journeying from the northeast. This is something you have no control over, so what can be done?

In this case, make a detour so that you arrive at your destination from a direction that is auspicious for you. This means making un-scheduled stops at cities along the way. So if you are traveling to Boston from London for instance, you can stop over in New York or Washington before going there.

Look at travel directions

If you are offered what appears to be a very lucrative new assignment or new job that involves a physical relocation, always examine the travel direction first as this will give you an idea of whether the new location will be good for you. When I was transferred to Hong Kong, for instance, it involved relocation for me from Kuala Lumpur. At the time of the transfer I did not check my directions so it was just as well when some years later I discovered that the relocation was excellent for me, which was why my nine years in Hong Kong turned out to be very rewarding from a financial and career viewpoint.

126 feng shui cures for travel obstacles

If you have no choice but to make an important journey from an inauspicious direction, you can minimize the harmful effects of this by taking a detour.

For a major move, it is recommended that you stay at least six weeks in your stop-off point to weaken the negative influences of the first part of your journey. However, as this is often not practical, below is a list of the small things you can do to dilute inauspicious chi when traveling from unlucky directions:

Wearing auspicious motifs or jewelry in gold such as the double circle, double diamond or bat when you travel deflects bad energy from the east and southeast.

Fresh flowers protect against bad energy when traveling from the southwest or northeast.

- From the south, drink one glass of water prior to departure; the numerology of 1 is important here, so only drink one glass.

- From the north, point a quartz crystal in the direction of north before leaving your home.

- From the west and northwest, wear red or light a red candle before leaving home. This symbolically negates the negative, or shar chi, coming from that direction.

- From the southwest or northeast, carry a bunch of fresh flowers with you as you leave the house. This symbolic energizing of the Wood Element keeps bad energy at bay.

- From the east and southeast, wear some gold on you on your travels. You can also hang a windchime in the east until you return from your journey, then take it down. This is also a good way to protect your home while it is empty, if you are away on holiday or a trip.

127

energize your chinese animal sign

Every animal sign in the Chinese zodiac has an associated compass location. Activating these areas of your home is a way to really personalize your feng shui.

To find your animal sign, you need to check out your date of birth in the lunar tables on page 215 to discover the sign you were born under. Then you can activate your personal "animal" sector of your home in two special ways:

1 Place statuettes or other attractive representations of your animal in the associated corner. Make sure that the animals are benign rather than ferocious looking, particularly for the dragon and the dog. Otherwise the good chi created by animal placement will be literally eaten up. It is even better if you can find objects made from the Element for your sign, for example, a ceramic ox or a wooden tiger would give your feng shui extra power.

2 Place symbols of the Element of your sign, such as a dog, boar or rat next to a water feature. However, the water feature should not constitute a toilet, sink, bath, or shower, as this has the effect of draining energy (as this is their function) rather than boosting it. So, if your kitchen or bathroom falls in the sectors relating to the dog, boar, or rat, do not activate with animal or water symbols as this area is inauspicious for you anyway, so you will only magnify belligerent chi by doing so.

Your animal sign direction and Element

Animal sign	Compass location	Element you can use
Rat	33.7 and 7.5 degrees	Water
Ox	7.5 and 37.5 degrees	Earth
Tiger	37.5 and 67.5 degrees	Wood
Rabbit	67.5 and 97.5 degrees	Wood
Dragon	97.5 and 127.5 degrees	Earth
Snake	127.5 and 157.5 degrees	Fire
Horse	157.5 and 187.5 degrees	Fire
Sheep	187.5 and 217.5 degrees	Earth
Monkey	217.5 and 247.5 degrees	Metal
Rooster	247.5 and 277.5 degrees	Metal
Dog	277.5 and 307.5 degrees	Earth
Boar	307.5 and 337.5 degrees	Water

128

how to activate the four important trigrams

In the next four Tips, I explain how to activate the four trigrams in your home. These trigrams collectively define the family, symbolizing the essence of the father, mother, son, and daughter.

Please note that the four important trigrams in any home are Ch'ien, which symbolizes the patriarch, K'un which signifies the matriarch, Ken which symbolizes the middle son, and Sun which signifies the middle daughter. Together these four trigrams represent the family unit.

Activating these trigrams means making certain that the four secondary directions of northwest (patriarch,) southwest (matriarch,) northeast (son,) and southeast (daughter) are not afflicted or missing, and are properly energized.

The family directions

These same four directions also stand for creating good patriarchal and matriarchal luck, which translates into money and relationship luck. The northeast signifies wisdom, and the southeast, wealth.

It is not always possible to ensure that all four corners indicated enjoy good feng shui and if this is the case with your home, what you can do is select a room where the family spends a great deal of time together. This can be the family room, the living room, or the dining room. So when you find it hard to have the four secondary sectors of the house properly energized you can, for instance, select the living room as the place in which to put the guidelines on the four trigrams into practice.

Using the living room to energize

Utilizing this room as a unit on its own to energize the sectors as indicated is adopting a powerful but little known principle of feng shui – replacing big chi activation with small chi activation. Instead of using the whole house to activate the four important trigrams, you can use one room to do exactly the same thing. This is perfectly acceptable in feng shui practice.

The four family trigrams

Ch'ien is for the father.

K'un is for the mother.

Ken is for the middle son.

Sun is for the middle daughter.

129

energize the ch'ien trigram for protection

So the first trigram and direction to activate is the northwest, and irrespective of whether this direction is favorable or not for the man of the house, you should still activate the northwest.

The good effect of doing this is that it benefits everybody in the home as this also means that the household has a head whose feng shui has been properly protected and looked after.

Using Earth energy

The northwest, being Metal, always benefits from crystal Earth energy (as Earth produces Metal in the Element Cycle,) so place a large crystal in this corner. Also place lights here to brighten the corner with good yang energy and to activate the special qualities of the crystal.

You can also hang a six-rod windchime as 6 emphasizes the lucky number of the northwest sector. Another way is to place a "mountain of gold" in this corner. There is an elaborate feng shui Taoist ritual to create the mountain of gold, but it is a secret practice. To simplify matters, place a picture of a mountain that looks gold because the picture has been taken at sunrise.

Mountains of gold hold great significance in feng shui. Finding such mountains is thought to be the ultimate in feng shui heaven.

130 activate the k'un trigram for family happiness

Activating the southwest will not only benefit the mother, but will also generate the luck of relationships for the whole family. When the mother is lucky, everyone benefits.

K'un is one of the most important trigrams of the Pa Kua and the southwest should not be missing or afflicted in the house. If the southwest is occupied by a toilet, then you should place a plant inside the toilet to destroy the afflicted Earth energy and then place bright lights just outside the toilet to enhance the Earth energy outside. Another way to deal with the toilet is to weaken the Earth energy inside the toilet with a five-rod windchime.

Activating the southwest also provides the household with a bonus in that it activates the marriage or relationship luck of all who live there, so that the children of the family who are of marriageable age will find good partners and the relationship between the father and mother will be strong.

131 trigrams that benefit your children

To energize these trigrams, boost the northeast (Ken) and the southeast (Sun) corners of the house. If they are missing, activate the equivalent corners in the living or dining room.

The northeast benefits the sons, and also signifies the luck of education and examinations. The southeast benefits wealth and growth luck.

If the northeast corner is afflicted by the presence of a store room or toilet, then hang a windchime inside to weaken the afflicted Earth energy. If it is in the southeast, then place a candle inside the toilet or create put some bright lights in there to drain the energy. Alternatively, paint the toilet red to exhaust the stagnated chi inside the toilet.

It is also a good idea to place a painting of a young man or portraits of the sons in the northeast and portraits of the daughter in the southeast, as this creates auspicious luck for the son and daughter of the family. This also works if the portraits face the northeast and southeast respectively.

5

special

feng shui

tips for

apartments

132 using your building's main entrance

When you are investigating the feng shui of an apartment, take the view that it is part of a building so that you begin by investigating its overall feng shui before doing anything else.

Whether or not your apartment will bring you luck depends a fair bit on the bigger picture and this must incorporate the whole building. In fact, feng shui masters adept at calculating the powerful flying star feng shui charts always use the entrance into the apartment building to work out their feng shui charts first, before studying the apartment itself. This is because the building's chi influences the luck of all its apartments.

It is rare for every part of a building to have completely bad or completely good feng shui. It does not work this way, because every building always has good and bad corners. The lucky and unlucky sectors of a building also do not remain constant in terms of luck, because feng shui is a dynamic phenomenon. Different sectors of a building take turns to be lucky and unlucky. This is a fundamental concept of the flying star feng shui, which manifests good and bad luck according to the building's orientation as well as the passage of time.

For apartments, note that the entrance and orientation of the building itself is more important than the entrance into the apartment.

Using flying star feng shui

Unless a building is seriously affected by symbolic poison arrows that hit its main entrance, or there are structures within its environment that cause it to be afflicted by environmental problems, the luck of a building and all its residents can be very accurately gauged and ascertained using the flying star method of feng shui.

So in the case of apartments, you should always assess the feng shui of the main entrance into the whole building before analyzing the apartment inside the building. When you know this, you can locate the lucky sectors of your home, which are given in Tips 134 and 135.

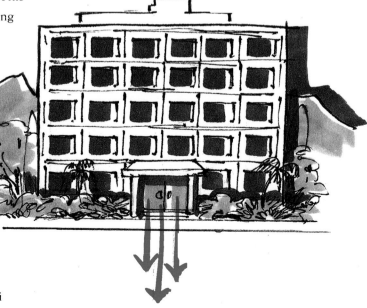

133

flying star identifies lucky sectors

It is worthwhile knowing flying star feng shui just to possess the expertise to work out the natal chart of your own home. This advanced formula is surprisingly simple.

For those of you who do not have the patience to do your own feng shui (let alone work out their flying star feng shui charts) you can scrutinize the summary of lucky sectors within homes, and offices, that is given overleaf.

How to use the flying star summaries

The summaries in Tips 134 and 135 are based on the outward facing direction of the main entrance of the building and applies only to buildings completed or renovated during the period of 7, i.e. between February 4th 1984 to February 4th 2004. In this period there are 16 different categories of houses. There are two categories for each of the eight cardinal directions (north, south, east, and west) and two categories for each of the secondary directions (northwest, northeast, southwest, and southwest.)

Within each of these homes the lucky sectors (expressed as compass directions,) have been identified. If your front entrance door is located in a lucky sector or if your bedroom is placed there then you benefit directly from the good luck in that sector for the entire period of 7.

Your best corner

Please note that usually the best corner is the corner diagonally opposite to the main door of every abode — this guideline is based on general feng shui principles. If you find that the lucky sectors identified by flying star principles are not diagonally opposite the main door, don't worry — you can still activate your general lucky corner and use your new flying star corners, too. All you are doing is fine-tuning your feng shui practice and applying the deeper secrets of the feng shui masters.

134 cardinal directions and lucky sectors

The lucky corners of buildings are based on the main door facing their orientations. Here the lucky corners of buildings facing south, north, west, and east are given.

Note that each compass direction occupies 45 degrees, and the secrets of the formula revealed below fine tunes the facing direction.

Buildings facing south

A period 7 apartment building facing south between 157. 5 to 172.5 degrees has three lucky corners, at the back, in the north and northeast sectors, and in the front south sector. The building's entrance is also auspicious. If the building is facing south between 172.5 to 202.5 degrees it has two lucky sectors in the front, that is in the south and southwest corners, and at the back in the north corner of the building. So apartments located in the lucky parts of the building will benefit.

Buildings facing north

A period 7 apartment block that is facing north between 337.5 to 352.5 degrees has two auspicious corners in the front of the building, in the north and northeast sectors and one lucky sector at the back in the south. Placing a waterfall directly in front of the building brings money luck to all the residents. If the building is facing north between 352.5 to 022.5 degrees, it has two auspicious corners at the back of the building in the south and southwest grids of the building, and the north entrance grid is lucky. Water in the southwest corner of any of the apartments in such a building will benefit the occupants' success luck.

Buildings facing west

A period 7 building facing west between 247.5 to 262.5 degrees has one lucky location in front in the northwest corner and one lucky corner at the back in the southeast corner, and both these corners will benefit from a water feature. If the building is facing west between 262.5 to 292 degrees it has two lucky sectors in front of the building in the west and northwest sectors, and one lucky corner at the back in the southeast corner. A water feature in the southeast or northwest of such apartments will bring financial success to occupants.

Buildings facing east

A period 7 building facing east between 067.5 to 082.5 degrees has one lucky sector in front in the east, where the main door is located, and one lucky sector at the back in the northwest. Place an aquarium in the northeast corner of the apartment itself (except if this is occupied by bedrooms.) If the building is facing east between 082.5 to 112.5 degrees, lucky sectors are located in the southeast and west of the building.

135

secondary directions and lucky sectors

In this Tip the lucky corners refer to houses whose main doors face the secondary directions – the southwest, southeast, northeast, and northwest.

As for the cardinal directions in Tip 134, here are the secondary facing directions for the period of 7.

Buildings facing southwest

A period 7 building facing southwest between 202.5 to 217.5 degrees has lucky sectors in the southwest in front of the building and in the back sectors, in the north and east. Water features (such as aquariums or ponds) placed in the north of the building or in the north corner of apartments will generate enormous money luck. If the building faces southwest between 217.5 to 247.5 degrees, then it enjoys plenty of money luck. The lucky sectors are the south and west at the front of the building and the northeast grid behind. Water placed in front of the building enhances the luck of the building.

Buildings facing southeast

A period 7 building facing southeast between 112.5 to 127.5 degrees has its lucky sector located in the center grid of the building, so bedrooms located here will have the best luck. If your apartment building faces southeast, between 127.5 to 157.5 degrees, energize good luck by placing water in the west corner of your apartment.

Buildings facing northeast

A period 7 building that is facing northeast between 022.5 to 037.5 degrees has two lucky sectors in the front of the building, at the north and east corners, plus one lucky sector in the southwest grid at the back of the building. Apartments in such a building can be made extremely lucky by energizing their east corners. If the building faces northeast between 037.5 to 067.5 degrees, the main door is lucky, and the lucky locations within the building are at the back in the west and south corners. Water features placed in the west of apartments inside such buildings bring good money luck.

Buildings facing northwest

A period of 7 building facing northwest between 292.5 to 307.5 degrees has a lucky central grid. The east corners are also luckier than the rest of the building. Apartments within such a building should energize with a picture of mountains or a dragon in their east corner. If the building faces northwest between 307.5 to 337.5 degrees it also has a very lucky central grid. So apartments within enjoy good feng shui. The west corner of this building is very lucky. Apartments will benefit from a mountain picture on their west walls.

136 activating the lucky sectors

There are many different ways to activate good luck for apartments, and feng shui practitioners really are spoilt for choice because of the variety of different methods that can be used.

I have discovered that the best way to activate for good luck, however, is to combine my knowledge of flying star feng shui with symbolic feng shui. When you can identify auspicious symbols, and you know how to place them correctly inside your home (be it an apartment or a house,) you will usually feel the difference very quickly. This is because you are using flying star to identify the lucky sectors of your home and doing whatever simple things are necessary to energize that sector by strengthening the chi there. You simply use the Five Element theory to do this.

Keeping healthy fish in an aquarium is a powerful water feature which can achieve good luck.

Boosting lucky corners

For instance, if your lucky corner is in the southwest, then knowing it is the Earth Element means that the sector will benefit from some bright lights or anything to do with Fire. This is because Fire produces Earth in the Element Cycle. Here's another example: if the north is your lucky sector, you can place Metal energy there which will enhance the Water energy of that corner. So the key to correctly enhancing any lucky corner is to place an object there that represents the producing Element of that sector (see Tip 81.)

What enhancers to use

Different items can represent the Elements. So you can use candles or lights to represent the Fire Element, coins or metallic objects to represent Metal, a picture of a waterfall to represent Water, crystals to represent Earth, and plants to represent Wood. However, note that these are only suggestions; use your creativity to think up suitable decorative objects to enhance the luck of your auspicious corners. Try to combine your knowledge of the Elements with your knowledge of auspicious symbols as well so you can always use lucky symbols for wealth, for romance, for health, and so forth to magnify these specific areas of luck.

137 some powerful symbols of good fortune

Feng shui offers a host of potent, auspicious symbols that you can use to promote good fortune in all areas of your life: wealth, romance, longevity, and career.

You can stimulate different types of luck using some of the more popular symbols of good fortune from the following list:

- Wealth luck – you can hide a few three-legged toads under the sofa, or have them seated on a coffee table looking at the door from an angle. This always works to bring in money-making opportunities. Another great wealth luck symbol is the gold coin or ingot. Placing a whole bowl of these wealth activators in your lucky corner will do wonders to enhance your prosperity luck.

- Longevity luck – place long-life symbols in your lucky corner. This usually also brings you the luck of health and wellbeing. Longevity symbols include pictures of the pine tree, the peach, or the bamboo. You can also have real miniature bamboo plants growing in your lucky corner to bring you this luck.

The money-laden sailing ship is a potent career booster.

- Career luck – place a ceramic turtle, hang a picture of a turtle, or place real terrapins in your lucky corner. This symbolizes the protective chi of this celestial creature. He also ensures longevity of tenure at your job. You can also hang a picture of your role model here to create the luck of powerful mentors who give you a helping hand at work.

- Romance luck – place any of the love energizers in your lucky sector. Mandarin ducks are a powerful activator and when placed in the lucky sector stipulated by flying star this brings excellent romance luck. The partner that it attracts into your space will certainly bring you happiness.

The three-legged toad brings in wealth.

138 toilets above the main door cause affliction

One of the disadvantages of living in apartments is that you have little control over the feng shui afflictions that come at you from apartments above you.

The most harmful affliction coming at you from above are toilets that are located immediately above your main door. If this affects your apartment, do try to use another door as the entrance and close this afflicted door permanently. If you cannot do this, place a bright light in the foyer area to symbolically lift the chi here. This cure, however, may not be very effective.

Another way is to create a second door further inside the apartment. This symbolically traps the bad chi between the two doors and, if you always keep this little space well lit, it dissipates the bad energy coming from the toilet above.

Toilets in the apartment above yours should ideally be above the toilets in your apartment.

Otherwise, there is always the danger that they may inadvertently be harming your feng shui. It is a good idea to find out if this is the case. For instance, if you or your family seem to be sick all the time, but your feng shui is fine, you may want to check if you are sleeping under a toilet.

A feeling of oppression

If you have no appetite, and constantly feel oppressed, there could be a toilet (or a heavy object) placed directly above you in the apartment above. If you feel like this, try moving your furniture around. Often simply shuffling your chair to another position can make you can feel better.

139 arrange your beds and tables for success

When it comes to arranging furniture inside your living and sleeping areas, try to position them so that you can tap into the auspicious directions of all members of your family.

Choosing the good directions that generate the kind of luck you want is also important. Check out your four auspicious directions from the charts in Tip 110.

Placing beds in good directions

For example, all beds should ideally be placed so that the head of the sleeping person is pointing to his or her success direction. If the sleeping person is a young person then the Fu Wei, or personal development direction, may be best. When you sleep is one of the best times to let yourself benefit from your auspicious Kua directions – this is because most people sleep for seven to eight hours a night. Let the chi that enters your head come from your good direction.

Good seating at the dining table

When you're eating around the dining table, it is an excellent idea to seat every member of the family according to their individual auspicious directions. When the dining table is arranged this way it becomes a powerful energizer of good luck. My advice, however, is that since this is the time when members of the family gather together to eat their daily meal, it is a good idea to tap into their Nien Yen rather than their Sheng

The entire family can be seated according to the Kua formula. Select the Nien Yen directions for everyone, so that family mealtimes become pleasant bonding experiences for all of you. The Nien Yen represents the luck of generations.

Chi directions (see Tip 110.) By doing this you collectively activate the family luck to bring fulfillment and happiness, and the continued wellbeing of the family as a complete unit.

Always seat yourself in a favorite sofa seat that has been positioned to face your best direction. This will ensure that you will always feel good and happy when people come visiting. Friends then also become a genuine source of good fortune. Never arrange your sofas in an L-shape.

140 remedies for overhead beams

Apartment dwellers are especially vulnerable to exposed structural overhead beams. As space is limited, beams are harder to remedy but flutes or bamboos should do the trick.

According to the general guidelines of feng shui, you need to avoid being hit by the sharp edges of pillars, stand-alone corners, tables, and other structures as these send out harmful cutting chi that can cause sickness and loss. It is also not a good idea to sit directly under exposed overhead beams, especially if these are heavy and seem to be pressing down on you.

Overhead beams

In apartments, this latter affliction becomes lethal, especially when the beams are structural beams. Imagine being on the receiving end of several floors of such beams! It is vital, therefore, to work out where these beams are and make sure you never place your bed, your dining table or your work desk directly under such structures. Moving furniture away is far more effective than simply hanging antidotes and remedies.

Sitting under beams

If you really have no choice but to sit under structural overhead beams then make sure that you hang hollow bamboo stems under them, tied facing each other at an angle. These pieces of bamboo should be tied with red thread which will give them added potency. Another popular cure

Hang firecrackers to symbolically dissolve the edges of overhead beams. Note that they should never be lit; their presence is enough to negate the oppressiveness that these beams create.

favored by Hong Kong masters is to hang a bunch of firecrackers on the beam as symbolically they destroy the beam.

141 improving the feng shui of studios

I have received many letters from young single men and women enquiring about improving the feng shui of studio apartments and one-room lofts. The answer is to demarcate the space.

As their home is simply one big room they have found it difficult to practice all the different methods of feng shui. In actual fact, however, studio apartments and especially lofts (because of their larger floor area) are simply so easy to feng shui, especially if they are a regular shape. So in this case superimposing the Pa Kua or the Lo Shu Square to identify each of the eight compass direction corners is a simple matter. Then it is only a matter of identifying the lucky corners and using them to position your bed and your work desk. Always try to arrange your apartment so that your key living areas fall in your lucky sectors.

Be careful with activators

Studio apartments and one-room lofts should, however, not be activated with plants or water features. This is because the room will include your bed, making the whole room your bedroom. So it is safer not to place water and plants here as these are considered to be potentially harmful in the bedroom. It is also important to make certain that any mirror placed inside the apartment does not directly reflect the bed.

These guidelines still apply if you have a "put down" bed that you pull down nightly from a wall cupboard, or you sleep on a convertible sofa bed.

The aquarium to the right of the bed should be removed as in this studio apartment the living area doubles as a bedroom, which should never contain a large body of water. The floor space is clearly demarcated by the screen, so the corners can be activated according to Element theory. Treat the bedroom/living as one room and assess the kitchen independently.

Positioning the bed

The bed should be placed to tap your best directions, and toilets or bathrooms need to be blocked from the view of the bed. Where possible, observe all the other feng shui guidelines that apply to homes in general but all the time be aware that the entire room is considered to be a bedroom. So remembering to observe bedroom taboos is very important.

142 boosting chi in two- or three-bed apartments

Apartments that have two or three bedrooms should take note of the flow of chi within their homes as a starting point to doing their feng shui. Let the flow of chi meander.

It is a good idea to have a small space directly in front of the entrance door for the incoming chi to settle before moving through the home. So placing plants and other auspicious decorative objects near the entrance space will cause the chi to pause – this is always a good thing. If you have a mirror here make sure it does not directly reflect the main door as it will send the chi straight out again. With ground-floor apartments, if it is possible place a water feature on the left-hand side of the door (inside looking out), as this will also cause the chi to pause and help it become auspicious. Just remember that water near the entrance of the home should never be a hole in the ground such as a sunken pond – a small fish bowl is ideal.

The auspicious bedrooms

The influential residents of the home – the husband and wife or mother and father, whoever is most important, should occupy bedrooms that are located in the most auspicious sector. Use a com-pass to get your bearings inside your apartment and then use the information and summary tables given in this book to identify your lucky sectors (see Tips 134–135) so that you can use them. Remember that using a bedroom, for example, activates the chi, but in rooms that are left empty or used little the chi can stagnate.

Slowing down chi

If you have a corridor inside the apartment, place decorative objects along the corridor, but try to do this without overcrowding it. Otherwise your chi gets blocked, which will then restrict your good luck. The idea is to slow down the flow of chi, as fast-moving energy in a straight corridor brings bad luck.

If you have a room at the end of a long corridor, you should definitely slow down the flow of chi to benefit the occupants of the bedroom or other room there. Place paintings on the wall, plants along the corridor, and keep the place well lit.

143 taboos in multi-level apartments

If your apartment is situated on two floors, always make sure that you never have the dining areas and main doors afflicted by toilets on the upper floors.

Always sleep on the upper floor, so position the bedrooms up there. If you have split levels in your apartment, make certain that the family eats on the upper levels and that the guest areas, such as the living room, are located on the lower levels.

Staircases should be by the side of the apartment and not in the middle. Slatted, or open, staircases cause wealth to seep through, so fill in open staircases for good luck. Circular staircases are lucky, but spiral staircases are not suitable for the insides of homes, and can be especially unlucky inside apartments. If you have a mezzanine floor in your apartment it is not a good idea to sleep on the halfway level.

Extra-high ceilings are fine, but only if your apartment is spacious and has the floor space to take the high ceiling. Otherwise, an imbalanced effect is created which causes chi to turn inauspicious, as it becomes forced into a funnel effect.

144 finding the place of prosperity water

The place of prosperity water in any apartment is the east, the southeast or the north of the apartment. These are the corners where water features could be beneficial.

Use a compass and mark out these locations and then select one of them to activate. Choose only one corner as having water in three corners will be too much and has the potential to symbolically drown you.

Tap prosperity water by placing a small aquarium or water feature in one of the corners mentioned above, making certain that your water is yang water, so that it is flowing or bubbling. Water that is filled with fish or with plants is also regarded as yang water, and this is most suitable for creating prosperity energy.

145 windchimes for doors facing elevators

A unique problem faced by apartment dwellers is when the door to the apartment directly faces a lift or elevator. This is like having a tiger stalk through your front door.

This can be a most inauspicious feature, and is especially bad if the elevator is a private one serving only your apartment and so opens directly into your apartment. It is considered unlucky, because the elevator shaft is directly facing your apartment or apartment door. This is a very dangerous situation which should be dealt with by looking for another door to use as your apartment entrance.

Workable solutions

If you cannot use an alternative door – often the case with apartments – then hanging windchimes directly in front of the elevator is one solution. Use a wooden chime rather than a metal chime and make certain the rods are hollow and preferably made of bamboo. This way the bad chi of the elevator shaft is distracted to some extent. Also, place a bright light over your main door to lift the energy.

Dealing with airwells

Another problem with apartments is that sometimes the whole building is built with an atrium or "hole" in the center of the block. If your apartment has this feature and the hole is at your back or near your kitchen, I strongly advise that you use a board to shield it from view. Also try to make sure that the wind, which circulates because of this arrangement, does not hurt your apartment. This is likened to the tiger chi leaping out at you from the hole, so when your apartment has an airwell, block it off – it is not good for you. Generally, "holes" signify loss of wealth. When placed in front of homes they are not so harmful, but at the back of the house they can be dangerous.

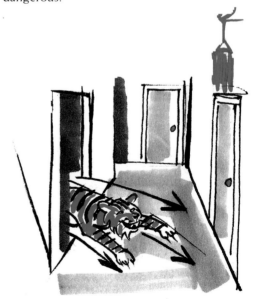

If your apartment door is opposite an elevator this represents an inauspicious hole afflicting your home, which is likened to the celestial tiger jumping out at you. Keep him at bay with metal windchimes hung by your front door.

146 outside foyers need constant light

Almost all apartments suffer from dim lighting in the foyer area just outside the front entrance. This usually causes the energy here to get very yin and stale.

When the chi that settles outside your apartment's entrance becomes stale, it causes good luck to disappear. To prevent this from happening, ensure that the yang energy has a chance to settle and accumulate. You can achieve this by installing bright lights outside your apartment door. Keeping the place well lit, especially with white light, is particularly good feng shui. If possible keep the light on – all day and night. Lights replenish yang energy.

147 use thick curtains to protect your balcony

When balconies of apartments are hurt or threatened by the edges of nearby buildings, killing energy is sent right through into the home and can be dangerous.

I recall when I was in Hong Kong, the first apartment I had was up on the Peak. It was very luxurious but its balcony faced a very large and singularly threatening round building that resembled a joss stick. I recall placing many Pa Kua mirrors which proved too puny to ward off the pernicious influence of that building. Nothing I did could ward off the bad effects of the building and I was constantly ill. I used heavy drapes to shut out the view of the building and felt better. But the view from my balcony also showed all of Hong Kong harbor in all its glory, and I often went out to enjoy the view. This meant, unfortunately, that I was allowing my apartment to become progressively afflicted.

In the end, I decided that it was a case of enjoying the view or suffering from increasingly bad feng shui. So I closed off the view permanently with heavy drapes. Only then did my feng shui improve. So if you have anything harmful aimed at you from nearby buildings, do shut it out with heavy curtains.

148 mirrors bring in auspicious views

If the view from your apartment is very auspicious, you can invite in the beauty of the great outdoors by using a wall mirror.

Perhaps if you are lucky enough to have a view of peaceful water, a field of green grass or a view of distant mountains, you can position your wall mirror to reflect, and symbolically welcome in, the positive chi of nature. This is especially auspicious if you can bring the view into your living room and not into your bedroom. Always remember that mirrors in bedrooms create yang energy; as bedrooms should be yin rooms, never use mirrors in bedrooms.

Expand auspicious views with mirrors.

149 hang crystals to catch sunlight chi

One of the most effective ways of bringing sunlight into your home is to literally make "rainbows" with crystals, which will enhance your feng shui enormously.

You can use balls of lead-faceted crystal to create these auspicious rainbows. Get those wonderful Austrian crystals that are used to make chandeliers and hang them in your windows to catch the light. This instantly breaks the light into a whole spectrum of rainbow colors. It is most auspicious and it brings in plenty of wealth and relationship luck. Make it a point to do this every time that the sun shines – not only will the energy of your apartment be enormously enhanced but it also allows yang energy to enter in its most benevolent form.

6

how to use

color in

interior

feng shui

150

the use of colors in feng shui enhancement

The use of colors in feng shui is based on two important principles that transcend all the different methods of feng shui, the theory of the Five Elements, and yin and yang.

Irrespective of which school of feng shui you are practicing, since the colors imply the application of the Five Element theory and the principle of yin and yang, they are effective irrespective of whether you are using form school or formula school of feng shui.

All the colors

Colors in feng shui cover the whole spectrum of rainbow colors and each takes on yin and yang aspects, depending on their shade and the amount of black or white that is present in them. As a general rule, the darker the color the more yin the color is said to be because of the preponderance of black. By the same token, the lighter a color is the more yang it can be due to the presence of white. Black is a yin color while white is a yang color.

Yang colors

Having said that please note that the color red (all the way to deep, dark red) is considered a yang color because implicit in red is the color of yang. Similarly, the color of yellow is also a yang color, and in fact the dark shades of these two colors symbolize good fortune manifesting in vibrant yang energy. A great deal depends on the kind of

red and the kind of yellow. Different types of red and yellow also suggest different types of good fortune and knowing which red to apply to your circumstances requires a detailed knowledge of the Five Element theory in conjunction with the symbolism associated with the different shades of these colors. In addition, it is useful to know that the colors red and yellow are highly complementary and when used together usually express the highest power, as well as the most auspicious and loyal attendants in life. Yellow is the imperial color of China reserved only for the emperor's family. The courtiers of high rank – those that serve the emperor directly – usually wear red. During important festivities and celebrations red comes into its own. So weddings, the birth of sons, as well as the new year, are all celebrated with the color red.

151

reds in the south bring vibrant yang energy

In using red to enhance feng shui energy, it is useful to understand which reds are auspicious. These are cinnabar, New Year red, and ox-blood red.

There are auspicious and less auspicious reds, so if you are a fan of red, it is essential to consider its variations. A very auspicious red is cinnabar red which is the red used to make many decorative carved jars and jugs that adorn a young lady's vanity table. It was believed the cinnabar red would help her make herself more presentable and attract a favorable suitor. As such, many of the old antique jars used for keeping creams, rouge, and powder were made in cinnabar red.

Then there is the New Year red, which is not unlike cinnabar red except it is a little lighter. This is the red of auspicious beginnings. A deeper, richer red is known as ox-blood red and this looks like maroon lacquered red. This color is said to imbue homes with the power of influence and authority. Many of the powerful mandarins exhibited a great fondness for porcelain of this color, and old Chinese mansions were usually decorated with huge ceramic vases, jugs, and so forth that were exquisitely fired in this color.

Red vases and porcelain

The use of this red in the form of vases and porcelain indicated that they were used with restraint. Too much was believed to cause blood to flow and so meant it had turned inauspicious, although red is not usually thought harmful.

Vases were usually kept in pairs.

If you use ox-blood red and cinnabar red in a modern decor, always have too little, rather than too much. For instance, use the reds as highlights in the south rather than as a solid color for walls or furniture. Screens are regarded very favorably by the Chinese as being a good way to introduce an important dominant color. So think about placing a cinnabar screen or a lacquered red screen in the south wall of your living room to attract vibrant yang energy. If you prefer, you can use the other auspicious reds, which include coral red and chile red. When it is energized this way, the auspicious chi in the south then creates the luck of recognition for the family patriarch. If you do not like using screens, try selecting curtains that have the same effect.

152

red and gold are auspicious attributes

Recognition luck is created by an auspicious use of red. Gold creates wonderful wealth luck, so by using these colors together you can activate awesome prosperity luck.

The color of gold is always auspicious as it signifies money. But gold also symbolizes the Metal Element and this can be harmful for eastern and southeastern sectors because Metal destroys the energy of Wood.

Wealth and prosperity

Combined with red, however, gold takes on a power of its own. Truly, the combination signifies extreme wealth and prosperity. In addition, gold and red is also a powerful combination that can destroy flying star afflictions caused by unlucky star number combinations. It is not a bad idea, therefore, to have some combination of gold and red inside the home and to bring this combination out during auspicious days.

The luck of red and gold

The meaning of red and gold together is also associated with high office, happy occasions, and wealth luck. It is for this reason that the Chinese always like this combination, and during the lunar new year wearing a red outfit with plenty of real gold is deemed to be wonderfully auspicious. It indicates a new year flowing with wealth and recognition. Inside the home the red and gold combination should never dominate whole walls. Instead, it is better to use it in subdued quantities as it works better as a highlight rather than as a dominant theme. Certainly it is not a suitable combination for bedrooms.

At Chinese New Year, gold coins are given as auspicious presents, always in multiples of three as three is a yang, or productive, number thought to bring wealth to the recipient.

153 the prosperity power of purple

There is a Chinese saying which goes something like "things are going so well that even red becomes purple." The implication is that purple is a powerfully prosperous color.

While purple does not enjoy the same royal reverence that it enjoys in the West, it is regarded as most prosperous. We are never certain if it is yin or yang as it exhibits characteristics of both, or if it signifies the Water or Fire Element. It is this surface ambivalence that makes it such an elusive yet extremely auspicious color.

When you paint your north wall purple you suggest its water, or its yin side. When you place purple in the south you are highlighting its vibrant yang side, but both these dimensions of purple are auspicious. So to use purple as your theme color is usually a good feng shui decision, if you can live with it. If you do not like purple, then pass on it; if you like it very much, by all means go for it. Personally, I would place purple in the north to let it signify water. When it is used in this way purple suggests prosperity luck.

154 purple and silver are wealth-bringers

The combination of purple and silver has been my signature combination through many successful business deals.

A Feng Shui master once told me that purple and silver spelt money and even sounded like money in Cantonese – ngan chee – which literally means "silver purple." I adopted the combination for my corporate logo and for the branding in my Dragon Seed department store, and within 18 months we sold the stores for a fat profit.

In the home, purple and silver can have a rather hi-tech look and is a combination that is most suited to Metal people, i.e. people born during years when Metal energy dominated. It is also suitable for homes that have a predominantly western orientation as the stress is on Metal energy producing Water.

155 green and blue bring in growth chi

The combination of green and blue suggests slow and steady growth, with none of the royal and more overpowering connotations of some of the other colors.

Blue with green is both harmonious and balanced, and is an excellent way of combining the colors in a room meant for growing children. It is an excellent combination for the sons of the family. This is because the chi created is growth chi which brings healthy growth and a happy family life. If you can get a picture of mountains painted in green and blue, it is a good idea to hang it behind you on a living room wall that is located in the east of the house.

The combination of blue and green is especially auspicious in the eastern corners of the home. This is because Water feeds Wood in the productive Element Cycle, making the plants grow. When you are applying this combination of colors, use more Wood and less Water, so green should dominate blue. A variation of this scheme is to use green with black (also representing Water) which not only looks good, but also brings harmonious chi together.

156 green and red create harmony and success

These wonderful, eternally popular colors of Christmas are not only a harmonious combination, but they also bring very happy luck.

Green is Wood, which fuels the flames of respect and honorable position attained by the head of the household. So green makes red strong. Wood makes the fire grow strong and big. To bring good fortune to the son (or sons) of the family, use the green/red combination after he has turned twelve. Introducing green and red color combinations into his south bedroom at this time could well bring him honors and respect. He will succeed at school and grow up well behaved. Green represents growth and red links with the completion of one phase of someone's life.

157 white and yellow attract the yang of light

Another powerfully auspicious combination of colors is white with yellow. This signifies the harmonious coming together of Metal produced by the Earth energy.

White and yellow portray wonderful vibrant yang energy, which can be very auspicious during the summer days. Once the sun comes out yellow gets magnetized, spreading warmth and good will. There are, of course, many shades of yellow, but if you use it as a combination in your home decor you might want to note that the color of imperial yellow, while being most auspicious, is simply not for everyone. It is believed that not everyone has the ability to wear imperial gold or yellow, and that it can invite illness. Likewise, not everyone can live in a room decorated in royal yellow. If you have decorated your room in gold or yellow and you cannot take the heaviness of these colors it is a good idea to immediately introduce walls of white to reduce the strength of the yellow.

Powerful colors

This principle of heaviness is a very Chinese concept, some even regard it as superstition, but it does seem to be rooted in reality. The colors which may pose this sort of danger to residents are yellow and purple. Indeed, I had a friend who experienced this. One day, in a moment of bravado, she decided to paint her living room a bright and glorious purple and immediately upon doing so she experienced a sudden surge in projects coming her way. As she was self employed, the new jobs represented greater income for her business.

Alas, it did not last. Her life chart did not indicate an ability to enjoy the palatial chi of purple and she soon succumbed to a severe illness that left her weak and in hospital for almost a year. It was only after her living room had been repainted back into a white color that she recovered. For her, purple was too overpowering – while it brought her extreme good fortune at the start, good turned severely inauspicious.

Softer shades

So if you feel intimidated by loud or overly auspicious colors, then decorate your rooms in light beige or white and then energize with decorative items made in the lucky color of your choice.

158 red and yellow make an awesome combination

These two colors are easily the most awesome in terms of the luck they can generate, as well as the afflictions they can cause.

When used correctly, and for the right people, red and yellow are a most formidable combination. To some people, however, the red/yellow double strength could be too heavy. It can cause unlucky residents who cannot bear their heaviness to become ill. This concept is very interesting. Sometimes, it can happen that the feng shui of a home is too rich, too yang, and too strong, so that although there may be nothing especially wrong about the feng shui it causes a bad effect in terms of chi backlash.

So it is advisable to be careful. Go warily at first. Test out the overall effect of the powerful red/yellow combination of colors slowly, beginning with small items placed within the vicinity of the space. If after a couple of weeks your luck seems to have started moving, then do not remove the color scheme, but become more ambitious in its use – try, for instance, using the colors in slightly larger areas.

Putting red and yellow in Earth corners

Use red and yellow in the corners of the home that correspond to them, so place red and yellow in the Earth sectors, which are southwest and northeast. The Earth sectors benefit from Fire energy as well as Earth energy. Putting red and

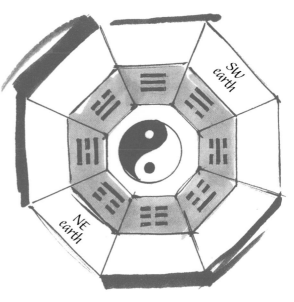

Yellow is the color for the Earth sectors, the northeast and southwest. Using red with yellow fuels Earth, bringing recognition.

K'un brings good fortune in relationships.

Ken benefits wisdom and scholarship.

yellow in these corners favors the flourishing of the family name. These colors also bring recognition to the family matriarch, thereby indirectly benefiting the whole family.

159 use black and white for harmony

The combination of black with white is always auspicious. This is because black signifies Water which is produced by white Metal in the Productive Cycle of Elements.

This means that the combination is harmonious and balanced and augurs well for the Water sector. Any place in the house which you feel will benefit from water will also benefit from a black and white combination of colors. Contrary to popular perception, black is not an unlucky color. It is also not the color of mourning. Indeed, black in many situations can be very auspicious as it represents the ultimate depth of Water energy.

A number of feng shui formulas focus on Water chi, because this is the Element that signifies money and wealth. Since many people use feng shui to magnify their wealth luck, Water becomes an important Element.

Place a black and white theme in sectors of the house that possess auspicious Water stars.

It is unnecessary to show too much black in your decor. Certainly, do not use black screens or curtains, but by all means use black as accent points or in accessories.

White, on the other hand, is a color you can use without any fear of overdoing it. This is because white contains within it all the colors of the rainbow and is therefore regarded as the ultimate color, as it possesses a balance of all colors. If you want to play safe, simply paint all your walls and ceilings white, and then use colors to bring out the chi of other Elements that are regarded as auspicious according to the compass corners you are dealing with. Remember that each sector representing one direction of the compass signifies an Element, which itself is represented by a particular color.

The traditional maze design can be used in single motifs or to create a repeat pattern in black and white to decorate your rooms.

160 black and green create growth and abundance

The combination of black and green is very similar to blue and green in terms of its effect. Water produces Wood, so black is excellent for the Wood sectors in the east and southeast.

If you use a significant amount of these two colors here you will benefit the children of the house – both sons and daughters equally. This is because the east stands for sons and the southeast signifies daughters. And because Wood energy means growth, the color combination brings out all the best in the chi of Wood. So let your colors be pure shades of the two colors. Choose a young, fresh green, rather than an old-looking, tired green. Always let your black be a clear undiluted black, pale looking rather than muddy. But once again do not overdo your use of black. Remember, too much Water is always bad as this is an Element that cuts both ways.

161 ceilings should be white

The best color for all ceilings is white as it signifies clarity and purity of colours. White is a very special and spiritual color.

White is made up of the seven rainbow colors, which in turn signify the seven chakras, or ancient points of energy, on the human body. It strikes a positive chord in every person and evokes moods and energy in accordance with each person's energy field. So for something as important as the ceiling of your home, which symbolically presses down on residents, use white to encourages the chi to rise.

White is also a yang color full of hidden life and positive spiritual energy. It is most auspicious indeed to have a white ceiling. If yours is a plaster ceiling do refrain from having too many patterns on the ceiling as anything pressing down on the residents below can become a potential secret arrow. It is better to have a flat ceiling with some decorative lines at the edges to signify the three yang lines of the auspicious trigram Ch'ien.

162 corridors should always have yang colors

Corridors are important conduit areas, as they channel the flow of energy within your living space. Do not make the mistake of ignoring the corridors.

The color you have here is as significant as the other rooms in your home. In fact, when the chi in the corridor is auspicious, slow, and harmonious, by the time it enters the next room it has become completely auspicious and benign. According to general feng shui principles, it is not auspicious to have a long corridor in your home. If you do have such a feature and you cannot do anything about it, read on:

- You can slow down chi by transforming the energy in the corridor. The most effective way of doing this is to use colorful paint, so use strong rather than pale shades. Select your colors according to the compass direction the corridor occupies – white for the west and northwest, green for the east and southeast, blue for the north, red for the south, and yellow for the southwest and northeast. Also, keep corridors well lit. If you do this you will already have created good energy within the home.

Colors for corridors

Determine which compass direction your corridor occupies. Then select the best color with which to decorate it, referring to the illustration.

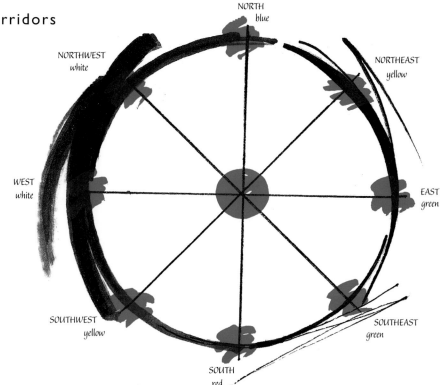

NORTH
blue

NORTHWEST
white

NORTHEAST
yellow

WEST
white

EAST
green

SOUTHWEST
yellow

SOUTHEAST
green

SOUTH
red

163

bedrooms are better yin than yang

Bedrooms should be dominated more by yin colors than by yang colors. So shades of blue and warm shades of earth colors are best.

Whatever you do, the bedroom should not be a place where colors cause the senses to vibrate too much as this will make it difficult for you to get to sleep.

Bedroom colors

Select colors for your bedroom according to your own personal Kua number (see Tip 107) – from the Kua you can tell which is your self Element and then you simply need to select colors that are auspicious for your self Element and avoid colors that hurt you. Use the Five Element Cycle to determine this (see Chapter 3, Tip 78,) look at the summary opposite, and work through the colors that are best for you. I have given here the colors that suggest the Element which produces your Element (the "self" element,) as well as the Element that is your alter ego. Based on the four pillars method of feng shui, the Element that produces you brings you wealth, while the Element that is the same as you is your partner. The fine-tuning comes only in the recognition of yin and yang in colors. So light colors represent yang energy, while dark colors signify yin energy. You will need your Kua number to tell you your Element. As women are yin, they should go for yang colors, while men, being yang, should go for

The yin yang symbol represents balance. Even when a bedroom needs to be yin, there will always be a seed of yang which defines the yin.

yin colors. This creates the balance that comes from the duality of the yin yang symbol.

Using the Kua number to determine the personal Element for purposes of enhancing personal feng shui, rather than using the four pillars method, highlights that this is feng shui enhancement, rather than that derived from fortune-telling. In truth, both methods can be used with success. However, when we use the Kua numbers to determine the Element, we have also taken account of the need to harmonize with the chi of surrounding space as well. In general, it is the Element that produces your self Element that usually is the most beneficial Element to activate.

Colors for wealth

KUA NUMBER	SELF ELEMENT	COLOR (FOR WEALTH)
I	water	white
2	earth	red
3	wood	blue or black
4	wood	blue or black
5	earth	red
6	metal	yellow
7	metal	yellow
8	earth	red
9	fire	green

Colors for love

KUA NUMBER	WOMEN: *Colors that bring you a partner*	MEN: *Colors that bring you a partner*
I	light blue	dark blue
2	light yellow	dark yellow
3	light green	dark green
4	light green	dark green
5	light yellow	dark yellow
6	white	gold
7	white	gold
8	light yellow	dark yellow
9	light red	dark red

164 floors need grounding energy

Colors for floors are best when they make you feel grounded, so it is always a good idea to use a stable color for the floor.

To a large extent this depends on the materials used. Stone materials such as terrazzo, marble, and granite, as well as their derivatives and combinations, suggest grounding energy. These give a solid base and those that are in Earth colors are the best. Always choose natural materials for floor coverings where possible. Do avoid floor patterns that have sharp points, such as star or obvious triangular shapes, because these become poison arrows on the ground which can hurt you more than you realize. Symbolically, they also look fierce and formidable and constantly suggest hostility. Therefore, keep floor patterns simple and welcoming, opting for soft, neutral shapes.

165 using blue on lower levels of your home

The color blue is synonymous with water and if you are a feng shui practitioner you should always be aware that water flows downwards.

As it is associated with water, blue is always meant for the lower levels and not for the upper levels of your home. This is why I strongly discourage blue roof tiles and blue ceilings, and why I actively discourage swimming pools on the roof levels or inside penthouses. Water at its zenith will simply flow down destroying what is below. So always keep blues of any shade on ground level. Blue is a yin color and it is very suitable for bedrooms at ground level as it is also very restful and calming.

Having said that, you should never place any kind of physical water such as an aquarium, in the bedroom although, of course, a glass of water by your bedside presents no problems. But blues on the walls, or used on your bedspreads and curtains, are perfectly fine. It exudes good yin energy without harming you.

7

special

feng shui

notes for

living areas

166 allocate space in the home carefully

Practicing your feng shui room by room becomes very easy as you progress, because the same principles apply in each room, although some rooms are more important than others.

What is important is to allocate space in such a way that lucky sectors never get wasted; or worse, get afflicted by a toilet or store cupboard being there. Instead, lucky sectors should be occupied by the patriarch or matriarch, or, where appropriate, by the sons and daughters of the family. The allocation of space within a home should reflect the family's aspirations.

The master bedroom and home office

Of all the rooms in the home, probably the most important is the master bedroom (and also the home office if you work from home.) It stands to reason that rooms which are used the most, should have the best feng shui. Only then will the family benefit from good feng shui of the home. So I wouldn't worry too much about getting every room of the home perfect in feng shui terms.

How to allocate rooms

The best method to use for allocating rooms is to work with the lucky sectors indicated by the flying star formulas. This is simply because these take account of the impact of time considerations. The lucky and unlucky corners of homes change over time. So those of you who wish to use this method might wish to pursue further research into flying star feng shui. Alternatively, you can refer to the table on lucky sectors given in this book to locate the lucky sectors of your home (see page 136.)

167

work with what you've got

The method you choose to apply in your home should rightly depend on the constraints of your own physical space, and the constraints of your budget.

Sometimes it is simply impossible to follow all feng shui recommendations. For example, you cannot use flying star feng shui if the lucky sector is occupied by the bathroom! In such cases you will have to check the Kua implications of the space that is available (see Tip 107,) and make some choices that will involve trade-offs. It is of no benefit whatsoever to fret. Feng shui offers you an analysis of why things may not be going right for you. If you can do something about it then do so, and if you cannot, then try to analyze it another way to see if you can tap another aspect of the chi that is flowing into your home.

A relaxed approach

You really have to work with what you've got. I cannot stress this strongly enough, and I look on this as the other great advantage of being familiar with all the different techniques available. Do not feel you absolutely have to apply flying star or Eight Mansions exclusive of each other. This is being dogmatic in your approach. All the methods of authentic feng shui can, and should, be used in combination with each other. Where you need to make a decision between two conflicting recommendations, choose the one which promises the kind of luck you feel you are lacking.

Feng shui is fun

Having said that, feng shui should be a fun practice. Do not be dogmatic about practicing feng shui. Remember that recommendations are very much based on the interpretation of ancient principles when living spaces and cities looked a lot different from today's environment. So while experience enables the feng shui master to interpret correctly most of the time, these interpretations are not cast in stone. There should always be room for creativity to permeate the practice of feng shui.

If you cannot tap your wealth direction with an aquarium in your living room, place the auspicious frog design, or three-legged toad or coins in the north to activate this sector. This type of frog brings good news rather than wealth.

168

using symbolism and rituals to best effect

When it comes to correctly activating special areas to attract specific kinds of luck this should engage your knowledge of symbolism feng shui.

Personally, I find this dimension of feng shui – using symbols to create good chi energy – to be the most fun of all, probably because it works so well and so fast.

I have discovered that when I combine my knowledge of lucky sectors, flying star feng shui, and Eight Mansions directions with feng shui symbols and rituals I really do get the most amazingly impressive results. In fact, often it just blows my mind when I see how fast feng shui seems to work. It is because of this that I am so passionate about practicing a combination of methods. I have discovered that when I use all the knowledge I have about feng shui it is simply not possible to discard one formula in favor of another. I have also discovered that no single method is more effective. Feng shui is a very complex practice where many different factors influence the quality of chi within the home.

The power of symbols

Peeling away at this huge body of knowledge constantly reveals fabulous surprises, and the power of symbols is what has really engaged my senses in the latter ten years of my study into feng shui. Also in recent years, when I had garnered up enough focus to use some of the rituals of feng shui which had been passed on to me, I found this even more amazing. Positive results were especially fast in coming when executed correctly. Using proper activators and doing it within an environment of already good chi energy also helped. All this is brought about by correct placement of doors, windows, rooms, and decorative objects.

Because of the speed at which some of these rituals work, I now think of this branch of feng shui as almost magical and I plan to write a whole book on these rituals.

The double happiness sign

The longevity sign

An alternative longevity sign

169

dealing with unlucky door orientations

Now you should be clear on how absolutely important the orientation of the main door is in big picture feng shui. This is dependent on a great deal of analytical feng shui.

It has a deep effect on the whole house, and it can also bring you luck from an auspicious direction. However, problems arise when, in investigating the feng shui of your home, you discover that the door is facing a direction that is unlucky for you and you cannot do anything about it. Naturally, if the way your house is oriented or designed allows you to change door direction then it is simply a matter of your budget and the inconvenience of undergoing a minor renovation. In this case I would ask you to think carefully and analyze the problem using the different methods suggested in this book before making changes. If you can find an efficient way of re-positioning the door such that you can benefit from good directions or if the new door orientation transforms, say your bedroom location into a lucky location

(based on the summary of lucky corners in page 70) then do go ahead.

Using your best direction

If you cannot change an unlucky door direction, and cannot find another door which can be "expanded" into the main door, then it is important that you make up for this by positioning your bed so that you sleep with your head pointing in your best direction. At the same time, camouflage the door by painting it so that it merges more easily with the wall. Some practitioners go so far as to make the door smaller in the hope that this will symbolically downplay the importance of the door. Personally, I do not know if this method works but it seems logical to reduce the importance of an unlucky door in this way.

170

the essential feng shui of the main door

There are some important points about a main door to observe if you want it to be the purveyor of good fortune chi for the household.

Follow these guidelines regardless of whether the door is lucky or not (for the patriarch or breadwinner.) However, if the door direction is facing say the total loss direction (see Tip 111) then activating it will only magnify the bad luck. So do use these guidelines carefully.

An effective main door

The main door can be made to be really effective in shepherding good chi into the home when:

- It is the largest door in the home, so it is obviously a main door.

- It is painted in a color that reflects its facing direction. So if it faces east or southeast it should be painted green for luck, or it should be left in a natural wood-grain finish. Doors facing this direction should never be painted white (this is because Metal destroys Wood in the Destructive Cycle of Elements.)

- Paint your southwest or northeast-facing doors yellow. The color to avoid here is green (this is because Wood destroys Earth in the Element Cycle.) Doors located in these compass sectors are best painted over and never left in wood-grain finish. If you must leave it in a wood-grain finish, then paint the wall yellow.

- Paint south-facing doors red, and avoid painting them black or blue (this is because Water destroys Fire in the Element Cycle.)

- Paint west or northwest-facing doors white, or use any of the metallic colors. Note that doors here should never be painted red.

A solid main door

Main doors are best when they are solid and open inwards, so that they bring the good luck inwards. Sliding doors are generally regarded as inauspicious if they are the main entrance into the home. If they are secondary openings into the home they are fine. Glass doors lack the security of solid doors and ideally should be avoided.

It does not matter if there are two leaves or a single panel to the door, or if one side of the door is larger than the other. Big mansions, however, fare better with grand double doors that swing open inwards.

Finally, to be lucky, doors should always open into, and open from, a "bright hall." In feng shui, a bright hall means a well-lit auspicious space around a main door. So inside and outside the door there should at least be a small foyer. A real hall would be even better. This allows chi to settle and accumulate on both sides of the door.

171

good fortune symbols in the living room

Once you are through the main door, the best part of your home to activate with good fortune symbols is the living room.

The main living area is a good place to have water, mirrors, lights, and so forth, because all family members will benefit. But in placing feng shui activators, you should observe some basic caveats.

Placing good fortune symbols

Do not place any mirrors opposite the front door, and in the living room, again, mirrors should not reflect the door itself. A mirror placed directly in front of the door will cause chi to fly out immediately. Even when it is reflecting a most beautiful scene, a mirror facing the door suggests a straight and deadly flow of chi.

Any water features (ponds, aquariums, or fountains) situated near the door should be on the left side of the door and never on the right side (the direction is taken inside looking out.) When water is on the right-hand side of the door, either inside or outside the house, the man of the family tends to develop a roving eye.

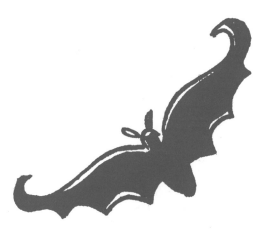

The bat is a precious animal as it represents good luck. It is therefore an auspicious symbol.

The symbol above is also auspicious: look out for both symbols and hang them up to attract prosperity luck.

172 energize every corner of the living room

The easiest way to activate all the corners of the living room is by enhancing the intrinsic chi of every one of the eight corners that represent the eight compass directions.

So in your mind you need to superimpose the Pa Kua symbol onto the living area. It is easier if you have a regular rectangular-shaped living room, but if you do not, simply take note of the protruding corners and missing sectors and deal with them accordingly. If there is nothing you can do about auspicious sectors being missing there is no need to worry about it. Instead focus on the areas of your living room that you can do something about.

Using a compass

Stand in the center of your living room and from there, using your compass, you can get your orientations. Find out where the north section of your living room is, then systematically make a note what direction each of the corners belongs to. Next see where your main living room door is located. The sector that has your entrance door is very important and you must make sure that it is not blocked in any way. Let the chi flow through doorways and entrances that make up your living area and especially your main door.

Work out the Elements

In all the other corners make a mental note of their respective ruling Elements based on the

direction that the corner is located in (see Tip 11.) You can then enhance the chi of each corner by having objects that reflect the Element of the corner; for example, putting plants in the Wood corners of the east and southeast, metal bells in the Metal corners of the west and northwest, earth-based objects (ceramics, crystals, and other such objects) in the southwest and northeast, lights or candles in the south corner, and water features in the north. The list can be much longer, of course, but this is where you can exercise your own creativity.

A money plant is a perfect energizer for the southeast corner.

173

get great luck from your lucky corner

While energizing each corner, you should locate the lucky corner of your living room and make sure that it is kept well lit and properly ventilated.

The lucky corner of the living room (and any room for that matter) is located diagonally opposite the door and this corner will generate greater luck if it is properly decorated in accordance with Element-driven colors and shapes, and then further activated by having lots of movement and activity there. Remember that yang energy gets automatically created in places where there is sound, movement, light, and human life.

Also, lucky corners always benefit hugely from auspicious symbols such as three-legged toads, lucky coins, and Gods of wealth and other Taoist deities being placed there.

Crystal in Earth corners

In the lucky corner of my living room, which is a northwest Metal corner, I have six round natural crystal balls (about 3in [76mm] in diameter.) This is to reflect the number of the corner (which is 6) as well as the fact that Earth produces Metal in the Element Cycle, so hence the crystal. Smooth, round crystals suggest smooth happy relationships, thereby keeping misunderstandings, angry words, and tempers to a minimum. They are also great for creating friendly energy. So I used the corner to activate harmony luck for all the members of my family. Because it was also the patriarchal corner, this also ensured that my husband,

being the patriarch, would benefit from good luck, thereby keeping him happy as well. The end result is a happy family!

The image of the Laughing Buddha brings happiness because he symbolically absorbs all your troubles.

174 livelihood luck in the dining room

Adjoining the living area will normally be where the family eats. So the dining room is also an important room which should focus on the family's livelihood luck.

Food on the table is always symbolic of livelihood and this is different from food in the kitchen. Food being cooked generates a completely different type of energy from food that is served on the table. Like a flower still in bud, food being cooked indicates food luck has not ripened yet. It is the flower that is in full

The mirror shown here is really quite inadequate as a dining room energizer. It needs to be larger so that it reflects more of the surrounding space, and particularly the members of the family who may be sitting at the extremities of the dining table.

bloom that suggests that luck has already arrived.

Which was why some years ago I was so amused when I was asked by some of my students whether placing a mirror in the kitchen to double the food being cooked was the same as placing a mirror in the dining room to double the food being served.

Mirrors in the dining room

In my books and lectures, I have always warned against placing mirrors to reflect naked flames and the stove in the kitchen. Mirrors in the kitchen therefore are dangerous features to have and I would never suggest placing them there. Mirrors in the dining room, however, are another matter altogether, as they can be most auspicious. Just do make sure that your mirror is large enough to suggest wealth and prosperity. Also, reflecting the members of the family at a meal is good feng shui. A large wall mirror would be quite perfect.

Mirror tiles

It is not a good idea to use mirror tiles in the dining area. And do make sure the mirror you use covers all of you and your family. Also try to ensure that it reflects the dining table and not another door, a toilet, the kitchen, or a staircase.

175 feature walls bring special good fortune

It is excellent feng shui to create a feature wall painted in a strong color that reflects your most important aspiration. Choose a wall either somewhere in the living or dining area.

So if fame and recognition are what you want, select a southern wall in the living or dining area, and then paint it bright red! This creates strong yang energy, so do this only on one wall, so it is not overwhelming.

If you want your career to take off, select a north wall and paint it a strong blue color.

If you want love and romance or a strong happy marriage, or good relations with everyone, then select a southwest wall and paint it a bright popcorn yellow, which is what I did to my southwest corners. They looked great, and instantly my family bonded even closer. It was amazing the way our lives became much happier. If you want outstanding examination luck for your children, then paint a northeast wall popcorn yellow.

If you want great good fortune for your children then paint a west wall golden. For good patronage luck do the same, but on a northwest wall.

Great health luck comes from a wood-panelled feature wall in the east, and good wealth luck comes from spring green on a southeast wall.

176 stimulating patronage luck brings heaven men

This sort of luck comes from a well-energized northwest corner. Place metal energy (six-rod windchimes or golden bells) in this part of the house, which stands for the leader.

The trigram of the northwest is the all powerful completely yang Ch'ien, which also signifies the divine luck of heaven. So when you activate this corner not only does it benefit the patriarch of the family, but it also brings good luck to all members of the household. So painting three solid lines to suggest the trigram is itself a powerful symbol to have in this corner.

177

activating feng shui for romance luck

For love to flourish in your life, you need to create the essence of good affinity feng shui in your home. Do this by protecting and activating the southwest – the universal corner of romance.

First use a good compass to mark out your southwest corner, then energize both the big chi southwest (the corner of the whole house) as well as the small chi southwest of each room separately.

Light up your love life with bright lights. When the southwest corners of your home are well lit, it attracts the energy of romance luck. Use white, red or yellow lights.

Boost the Earth Element

Use a cluster of natural quartz crystals to simulate the Earth Element. Crystals carry the excellent chi of the earth. Place the cluster on a table in your southwest corner. Also place a pair of mandarin ducks in this romance corner of your room. Make sure they are proper mandarin ducks and not mallards as the latter are notoriously unfaithful to their spouses! Mandarin ducks and geese on the other hand are well known for being faithful until they die!

If there is a toilet in your southwest corner, your love luck becomes seriously afflicted. Hang a five-rod windchime near the toilet, paint the inside of the door a bright red or hang a large mirror on the outside of the door. If your southwest corner is missing, you can still activate its chi by focusing on the southwest of your living or dining room. This creates the small chi, which is just as powerful as the big chi of the whole house.

Family luck

In feng shui, romance, love, and marriage are all part of family luck. Life is considered incomplete when this is missing. Feng shui can enhance romance in your life and bring you a life partner, but it is not for the frivolous. Unless you are ready for a commitment, don't energize for love. Activating love feng shui brings marriage opportunities and causes marriage luck to ripen. But it does not guarantee a perfect match – that totally depends on your karma.

178

activating strongly for for career luck

There is a universal career corner applicable for everyone which can be activated to benefit careers. This is in the north corner of your living room.

If this corner is properly activated with moving water, it creates excellent career luck for the residents of your home.

The trigram for the north is Kan, which represents a situation of entanglement and perpetual danger. It indicates that career people should always have the north sector guarded, so they never fall victim to intrigues.

Protective symbols

All ambitious career people should protect their careers and their career luck by either having real tortoises (or terrapins) swimming happily in a pond or aquarium in the north, or at least having a turtle image there. Another excellent idea is to keep a pet terrapin in your office. Keep him on a table or in a cupboard behind you, this ensures that precious turtle energy, which gives continuing protection from office politics, will always be with you.

Special symbols

The north sector of both your home and office will benefit from the placement of a water feature because the north belongs to the Water Element. Installing a mini fountain, an aquarium, or a even a small pond in the north brings excellent career luck.

Special bells, which are cast from seven types of metals (including gold and silver,) symbolize high positions. If you are after a promotion or are in the running for a particularly important job, ringing this bell every day in the north or northwest should enhance your chances.

In the old days, Chinese court officials wore embroidered insignias of auspicious symbols on their chests to signify their high rank. The closest equivalent of these auspicious power symbols would be ties for men and scarves for women; and good fortune jewelry for both.

Look for ties, tie pins, and cufflinks that feature auspicious symbols. For career luck, the most auspicious symbol would be the celestial dragon. Choose discreet designs and prints of the dragon. Wearing dragons or any celestial symbol in an overpowering fashion will cause imbalance and bad luck. Other significant and powerful symbols, which can be activated for upward mobility luck in your career, are the legendary unicorn, the chi lin, and the celestial phoenix. Wear these symbols to generate their heavenly chi.

The phoenix always brings in new opportunities. This is the creature that you must activate when you are down, unemployed, and jobless. It is an exceptionally good symbol to help you. Hang a painting of the phoenix in the north or wear a phoenix ring.

179 for wealth luck, protect against poison arrows

Create the essence of prosperity chi in your home by always protecting against secret poison arrows and activating all your wealth corners.

When enhancing income luck, protection against bad feng shui caused by killing chi is an important first step in the practice.

Looking out for the sources of bad chi or killing breath means developing awareness of things sharp, pointed, and hostile that hit your home, your main door or your eating, sitting, and sleeping places. First, always protect your main door. Straight roads, driveways, and footpaths should not be pointing directly at the door. Place a Pa Kua mirror above the door outside the door directly facing the straight road. Use the same mirror if the pointed triangle of a roofline is directly facing your front door, or when a single tree, a lamp post, or a tower is sending killing energy straight at your main door.

Tall buildings

More serious poison arrows come in the form of tall imposing buildings, especially if the edge of the building faces your main entrance. Such imposing sources of killing breath have to be blocked from view with trees and high walls.

If you want prosperity, never place the stove in the northwest corner of your kitchen. In addition to other manifestations of bad luck, this also causes you to lose your wealth. In feng shui terms this creates fire at heavens gate.

Let your food be cooked using energy that comes from your wealth direction. This means that your energy supply should enter your stove from your Sheng Chi direction (or that at least the plug faces in that direction.) Also, place your microwave, toaster, and electric kettle with their plugs pointing in this direction (see Tip 110) if you want prosperity luck.

When sitting down to eat at the dining table, ensure you are facing your Sheng Chi or wealth direction. Use a compass to check that this is your daily sitting orientation, but also ensure you are not being hit by inauspicious energy around you.

180 boosting for good health and a long life

In feng shui, good health means longevity. The Chinese attitude towards illness is that prevention is always better than cure.

This attitude is reflected in every phase and aspect of feng shui practice, so that having good health is a vital benchmark of good feng shui. So families that live in homes with good feng shui should live to a ripe old age and be generally free from life-threatening diseases.

How to ensure good health

There are several ways to ensure good health. The most important is to guard against being hit by the sharp edges of corners and beams when you sleep. If you are presently in such a situation, then try to move your bed away so you are not in the direct line of fire, or if it is not possible, then hang two bamboo stems tied with red thread or red ribbon against the edge of the beams or corners.

Guard against bad stars

The second way is to make sure you observe the warnings given in the next chapter about being hit by annual illness stars. Indeed, feng shui masters believe that the main cause of severe illness occurs when people get hit by the intangible chi of illness stars. So it is worthwhile observing this feng shui warning.

Always guard against the deadly five yellow and the illness star number 2. Both these numbers 2

When there are exposed beams above your sitting or sleeping locations, hanging two flutes will dissolve the effect. Place them in a shape like the angle of an "A," and about 6in (15cm) apart. Otherwise, you can suffer from migraines and headaches.

and 5 bring severe illness afflictions when they feature in the annual Lo Shu charts. It is for this reason that the Chinese are so fond of their Almanac. This book of auspicious and inauspicious days lists all the equivalent days and months which are hit by these numbers, so that if you have this Almanac you can simply calculate the danger days when illness and accidents could strike.

The third method of activating health luck is to display at least one of the symbols of longevity – the bamboo, the peach, or the pine tree. All of these can be displayed as paintings in the home. The Chinese, however, are especially fond of their longevity deity called Sau. He is an old bald-headed man who is often shown carrying a staff and a peach and followed by the deer – a symbol of longevity. His presence in your home brings wonderful energy. Invite him in!

181 the benign elephant for children luck

Children luck is the other all-important manifestation of good feng shui. It was believed in the old days that unless you had sons to carry on the family name, descendants' luck was sorely missing.

In those days, families would adopt sons if there were no natural sons. And not giving their husbands sons was usually sufficient reason for the man to take a new wife. That was of course in the old days. Today, women exert a strong influence over the family's wellbeing and having daughters is considered excellent for good descendants' luck. In fact, I only have one daughter but I consider myself very blessed with descendants' luck indeed, although it took us many years and feng shui help before we finally conceived Jennifer.

The early years of marriage

In the earlier years of my marriage after I discovered feng shui (I have been married to the same guy for over 35 years) I arranged for us to sleep with our heads pointing to my husband's descendants' luck direction. In fact, it was only after we had done this that we conceived Jennifer, and she was born after we had been married for ten years. She was the reason why I became so passionately interested in feng shui and how I got so hooked on it so early on in life.

The descendants' luck direction

To sleep in your husband's descendants' luck direction means tapping into his Nien Yen

The benign elephant brings descendants' luck.

direction (see Tip 110) when he sleeps. This is also the family and romance direction based on Eight Mansions. It is important for me to clarify that for couples wanting to use feng shui to help them conceive, this is the direction to use even if it is bad for the wife!

While sleeping in this correct direction you can also place an image of a benign elephant by the bedside as this is said to bring good children luck. And then as the children grow let them sleep, do their homework, and eat while tapping into their good directions. You can never start too young when it comes to feng shui. If you are blessed with good feng shui from a baby, you already have a good start in life. So if you are a parent, take note of this.

8

taking note

of annual

afflictions to

your feng shui

182

overcoming the afflictions of time

Even if you know nothing about the influences of flying stars, you can be aware of the year and the month that "bad" stars will afflict certain corners of the home.

This aspect of feng shui has to do with the way the feng shui of any space gets affected by the passage of time. The Chinese always pay equal attention to space and time dimensions when it comes to reading the influences of intangible forces that affect their wellbeing and luck. This requires knowledge of period cycles and flying star charts which need a complex arrangement of numbers around the Lo Shu grid. This method of feng shui also contains a predictive element and is not easy to learn.

The effects of the flying stars

For the amateur practitioner who does not know about flying star charts, what you do need to know is when and how the annual and month stars affect the feng shui of your home. You can incorporate this into your practice without knowing the flying star formulas.

Basically, we can identify three major types of bad flying stars that have the potential to bring afflictions, negative consequences, illness, loss, and accidents to members of your household. It is important to protect yourself from these influences with timely and often easy remedial action, but first you need to recognize where and when these bad stars will hit your home over the coming few years.

The three types of afflictions

These afflictions are:

- The affliction caused by the appearance of the star called the Grand Duke Jupiter.

- The affliction caused by the star of the Three killings.

- The affliction caused by the annual and monthly star called the Deadly Five Yellow.

These afflictions move around the compass chart each year and, according to flying star texts, there is a simple way of locating where they fly into each year, based on the movement of the earthly branches of the Chinese Hsia calendar. If unfamiliar with this calendar, refer to the following pages which explain the locations of the three major afflictions.

Take note of where they are each year and do not forget to take safety precautions to overcome and appease these afflictions at the start of each lunar new year. This way you will be protecting yourself from the star's bad influence. I cannot overstress the importance of paying attention to these time afflictions of feng shui. Usually, they have a great impact on your life because when they hit you, the effect is often far reaching.

183

the grand duke jupiter and how to appease him

Once you know where he is located, make certain you do not incur his wrath by sitting in a direction that directly faces his direction. This means you are confronting him and you must never do that.

You must never face the Grand Duke Jupiter directly when you sit, work or eat. If you do, misfortune befalls you even if that happens to be your best direction according to the Kua formula. Nor should you disturb his place with excessive noise, banging, digging, or renovations. If you do, the consequences are that you could get sick, suffer losses, lose out on important deals and opportunities, and generally feel rather sickly. So do make an effort to determine his location each year.

The Grand Duke Jupiter's location

- In 2001 is in the south, southeast (place of the snake)

- In 2002 is in the south (place of the horse)

- In 2003 is in the south, southwest (place of the sheep)

- In 2004 is in the west, southwest (place of the monkey)

- In 2005 is in the west (place of the rooster)

- In 2006 is in the west, northwest (place of the dog) and so on.

The Grand Duke's locations during each of the twelve animal years of the lunar calendar follow

the exact compass location of the animal year, so that in 2001, for instance, the Grand Duke resides in the compass location of the earthly branch of the animal snake, which means the fifteen degrees defined as south, southeast. The direction of the Grand Duke is shown in the illustration below – note how he moves in a clockwise direction around the compass.

This chart, showing the 12 earthly branches of the 24 mountains, shows the movement of the Grand Duke Jupiter.

184   how to confront the three killings

The Three Killings direction is also known as the Saam Saat. You must never have the Three Killings direction behind you in any year.

You should always confront it boldly, otherwise it sends three types of misfortunes to disturb and make your life miserable. So it is good feng shui practice to take note of where the Three Killings is located every year.

In 2001, which is the year of the snake, note that the Three Killings is in the east and you must not sit with that direction behind you. This means you should not sit facing west.

This holds even when the east is your best direction. You may, however, face the Three Killings directly. This means that in 2001 you can sit facing east. Confronting the Three Killings will not hurt you, but having it behind you will. In the year of the horse, in 2002, the Three Killings is in the north, so in that year you must not sit with the north behind you. It is far more advantageous to sit directly facing north, thereby facing the Three Killings head on.

House renovations

When you are planning to do house repairs and renovations you must not do it in sectors that house the Three Killings. So in 2001 this means you should not undertake any renovations in the eastern part of your house You may, however, undertake renovations in sectors that are opposite the Three Killings.

The Three Killings' direction

This always occupies only the cardinal sectors north, south, east, and west. So this is an affliction that covers 90 degrees of the compass. Here is the summary of where it flies to each year. Take note of these afflicted directions, and follow the advice given of never having your back to this direction and never disturbing it with renovations. If you have inadvertently disturbed the three killings, note the remedies given.

Remedies for the Three Killings

- In ox, snake, and rooster years the Three Killings is in the east (2001, 2005, and 2009.) Place a curved knife in the east during these years.

- In pig, rabbit, and sheep years the Three Killings is in the west (2003, 2007, and 2011.) Place more bright lights in the west in these years.

- In monkey, rat, and dragon years the Three Killings is in the south (2004, 2008, and 2012.) Place a large container of yin (i.e. still) water in the south to overcome the affliction.

- In dog, horse, and tiger years the Three Killings is in the north (2002, 2006, and 2010.) Place three large boulders in the north during these years.

185 Exhausting the deadly five yellow

The Five Yellow, which is also known as Wu Wang in Chinese, is considered a very harmful affliction that in certain years can cause untold damage to a family or a company that is directly hit by it.

This happens if the main door of the house or your bedroom is located where the star resides in any particular year. This is because each act of opening and closing the door, or any kind of activity in the place of the wu wang will simply activate its bad vibrations and will bring about misfortunes.

Like the other two afflictions the Five Yellow changes place each year, and where he is located in that year you must not undertake the following:

- You must not dig the ground.
- You must not disturb that part of the land or house in any way.

If the Five Yellow is disturbed it brings loss of wealth, loss of employment, accidents, injuries, calamities, robbery – and sometimes even death. The Five Yellow can take the form of the year star or the month star and when they occur in the same location at the same time, anyone residing in that corner of the home will immediately get ill. Of the two, however, the year Five Yellow is potentially the most dangerous, so my strategy has been always to prepare myself at the start of each year. I do this by weakening the Five Yellow in the location where he is each year. In the year 2001 the Five Yellow is especially dangerous because he has flown into the Southwest sector (whose Element is also Earth, just like the Five

Yellow.) Here the Five Yellow's energy has been strengthened by the Element of the sector itself. To overcome the energy of this star, the best remedy is to place a six-rod, all-metal windchime here. Metal energy, and especially yang metal, which moves and makes sounds, will seriously weaken and exhaust the Five Yellow thereby reducing its harmful effects.

So my advice to all feng shui practitioners is to always have a couple of all-metal windchimes handy and to hang this windchime according to where the Five Yellow flies into each year. So in 1999 the windchime should have been hung in the south of your house, in 2000 it should have been in the north. In 2001 you must have wind chimes in the Southwest, especially by the main door. Note the place of the Five Yellow in the years 2001 and beyond and that it occupies 45 degrees of the compass:

- In 2001 the Five Yellow is in the southwest.
- In 2002 it is in the east (where it is less harmful.)
- In 2003 it is in the southeast (where the Wood Element keeps it under control.)
- In 2004 it flies to the center of the home where it becomes ferocious once more.
- In 2005 it flies to the northwest where once again it is under control.
- In 2006 it flies to the west where it is also under control.

186 flying star in 2001 — the year of the snake

The year 2001 is the year of the snake. Note that the afflicted sectors in any house or building are the southwest, the east, and parts of the east/southeast.

These afflicted sectors are indicated in the feng shui chart of the year 2001 below — everyone should take note of the things to do as precautions against the afflicted sectors for 2001. From the chart here are some crucial things to put into place or take note of in the lunar year 2001 starting from February 4th:

- Place a six-rod wind chime in the southwest corners of your home to weaken the effect of the Five Yellow. If your main door is located here be extra careful. Better to use another door if possible. If your bedroom is here, try to move to another bedroom.

- Do not undertake any renovation work in the southwest, east, and also in the place of the Grand Duke, i.e. the fifteen degrees that make up its location in the east/southeast.

- Note also that the south is the place of quarrels and misunderstandings, so try to keep this corner quiet. Do not play too much music there and definitely do not have a windchime in the south this year.

- The illness star 2 is in the northeast sector of your house so place windchimes in this corner. Windchimes also weaken the 2 star.

- The auspicious sectors of homes will be the center of the

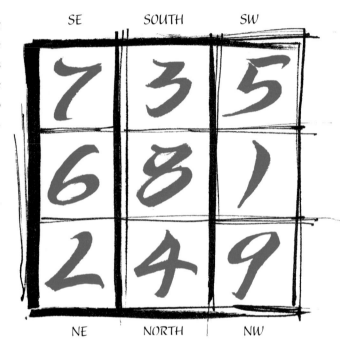

This is the annual chart for 2001. Note the deadly Five Yellow is in the southwest, the Three Killings is in the east, and the Grand Duke Jupiter is in the south/southeast.

home so do spend time eating in as this will be more auspicious than eating out this year.

- Place crystals in the northwest this year to benefit the patriarch of the family.

- Energize the southeast with plants and fresh flowers to enhance the income luck of the sector this year.

187

flying star in 2002 – the year of the horse

The year 2002 is the year of the horse. The afflicted sectors of any house or building are the east, the north, and parts of the south.

These afflicted sectors are indicated in the feng shui chart here which is the chart for 2002. From the chart, here are some of the crucial things to put into place or take note of in the lunar year 2002 starting from February 4th:

- Place a six-rod windchime in the east corners of your home to weaken the effect of the Five Yellow. If your main door is located here be extra careful. Use another door if possible. If your bedroom is here, relocate it if you can.

- Do not undertake any renovation work in the east or north, and also in the place of the Grand Duke i.e. the fifteen degrees that make up its location in the south.

- Note that the north is also the place of quarrels and misunderstandings so keep this corner quiet. Do not play too much music here and definitely do not have a wind-chime in the north this year. Instead place a large bowl with still water here to absorb all the bad luck of this sector.

- The illness star 2 is in the south sector of your house so place windchimes here to weaken it. In addition, use a big bowl of water to weaken the fire element of this corner.

- The auspicious sector in any home this year is the north-west which benefits from the number 8 star, so it's a good idea to energize the northwest to benefit the master of the house. Place lots of gold coins here, but avoid water.

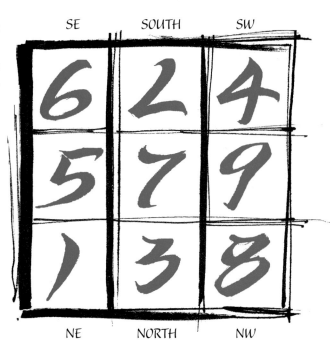

SE	SOUTH	SW
6	2	4
5	7	9
1	3	8
NE	NORTH	NW

This is the annual chart for 2002. Note that the deadly Five Yellow has flown to the east and the Grand Duke Jupiter has flown to the south.

- The southeast is also very lucky with the 6 star. So activate with a water feature here. The best feature is an aquarium which will bring good luck to this sector.

- Energize the southwest for good relationship luck with crystals and lights.

188 essential symbols to keep inside the home

There are several powerful symbols that you can place inside any home. In feng shui, symbols serve three different but important functions:

- To be protective.
- To act as effective remedies against intangible afflictions.
- To activate good chi and attract good fortune.

It is excellent feng shui practice to have all three types of symbols in the home which enable you not only to energize for good fortune, but also to protect against both tangible and intangible afflictions. So in this final point I would like to make strong recommendations for you to keep the following symbols handy inside the home:

- Always keep a good stock of six-rod, all-metal wind-chimes because these are simply so effective at fighting against the deadly flying star afflictions. For instance, follow where the five yellow star flies to each year and move your windchime along with it to control it.

- Keep a large urn available to hold still water. This is a very effective feng shui remedy against quarrelsome stars and noisy neighbors who may be giving you and your family a hard time.

- Keep a pair of Fu dogs as a protective symbol in the home. Place them at the front door on the outside looking out.

- Keep an image of the laughing Buddha which symbolizes happiness.

- Keep an image of the tortoise at the back of the home to symbolize longevity chi in the home. The tortoise is a powerful symbol.

Finally, make sure that you always have at least one wealth symbol in your living room. This can be the three-legged toad or the even more effective sailing ship loaded with a cargo of gold ingots.

Different feng shui cures and energizers

If you follow the different ways mentioned in this book you will have great feng shui without having to resort to massive renovation work. Use what you've got and understand that it is never possible to have one hundred percent good feng shui in your home. If you cannot change your home's orientation, then simply make sure your sleeping or working direction is auspicious to make up for it. Make your living space as regular, balanced, and harmonious as you can in terms of shapes, colors, and orientations. Do the best you can. In this book you will have found alternative ways to activate for good luck. There is no necessity to follow everything. But do guard against bad feng shui at all times. The key to having great feng shui is to make sure killing energy never hits, and then to progressively activate for good luck.

lunar

calendars

and index

ANIMAL	WESTERN CALENDAR DATES
RAT (water)	Feb 18, 1912 – Feb 5, 1913
OX (earth)	Feb 6, 1913 – Jan 25, 1914
TIGER (wood)	Jan 26, 1914 – Feb 13, 1915
RABBIT (wood)	Feb 14, 1915 – Feb 2, 1916
DRAGON (earth)	Feb 3, 1916 – Jan 22, 1917
SNAKE (fire)	Jan 23, 1917 – Feb 10, 1918
HORSE (fire)	Feb 11, 1918 – Jan 31, 1919
SHEEP (earth)	Feb 1, 1919 – Feb 19, 1920
MONKEY (metal)	Feb 20, 1920 – Feb 7, 1921
ROOSTER (metal)	Feb 8, 1921 – Jan 27, 1922
DOG (earth)	Feb 28, 1922 – Feb 15, 1923
BOAR (water)	Feb 16, 1923 – Feb 4, 1924

* start of 60 year Cycle

RAT (water)	Feb 5, 1924 – Jan 23, 1925
OX (earth)	Jan 24, 1925 – Feb 12, 1926
TIGER (wood)	Feb 13, 1926 – Feb 1, 1927
RABBIT (wood)	Feb 2, 1927 – Jan 22, 1928
DRAGON (earth)	Jan 23, 1928 – Feb 9, 1929
SNAKE (fire)	Feb 10, 1929 – Jan 29, 1930
HORSE (fire)	Jan 30, 1930 – Feb 16, 1931
SHEEP (earth)	Feb 17, 1931 – Feb 5, 1932
MONKEY (metal)	Feb 6, 1932 – Jan 25, 1933
ROOSTER (metal)	Jan 26, 1933 – Feb 13, 1934
DOG (earth)	Feb 14, 1934 – Feb 3, 1935
BOAR (water)	Feb 4, 1935 – Jan 23, 1936

ANIMAL	WESTERN CALENDAR DATES
RAT (water)	Jan 24, 1936 – Feb 10, 1937
OX (earth)	Feb 11, 1937 – Jan 30, 1938
TIGER (wood)	Jan 31, 1938 – Feb 18, 1939
RABBIT (wood)	Feb 19, 1939 – Feb 7, 1940
DRAGON (earth)	Feb 8, 1940 – Jan 26, 1941
SNAKE (fire)	Jan 27, 1941 – Feb 14, 1942
HORSE (fire)	Feb 15, 1942 – Feb 4, 1943
SHEEP (earth)	Feb 5, 1943 – Jan 24, 1944
MONKEY (metal)	Jan 25, 1944 – Feb 12, 1945
ROOSTER (metal)	Feb 13, 1945 – Feb 1, 1946
DOG (earth)	Feb 2, 1946 – Jan 21, 1947
BOAR (water)	Jan 22, 1947 – Feb 9, 1948
RAT (water)	Feb 10, 1948 – Jan 28, 1949
OX (earth)	Jan 29, 1949 – Feb 16, 1950
TIGER (wood)	Feb 17, 1950 – Feb 5, 1951
RABBIT (wood)	Feb 6, 1951 – Jan 26, 1952
DRAGON (earth)	Jan 27, 1952 – Feb 13, 1953
SNAKE (fire)	Feb 14, 1953 – Feb 2, 1954
HORSE (fire)	Feb 3, 1954 – Jan 23, 1955
SHEEP (earth)	Jan 24, 1955 – Feb 11, 1956
MONKEY (metal)	Feb 12 ,1956 – Jan 30, 1957
ROOSTER (metal)	Jan 31, 1957 – Feb 17, 1958
DOG (earth)	Feb 18, 1958 – Feb 7, 1959
BOAR (water)	Feb 8, 1959 – Jan 27, 1960

ANIMAL	WESTERN CALENDAR DATES
RAT (water)	Jan 28, 1960 – Feb 14, 1961
OX (earth)	Feb 15, 1961 – Feb 4, 1962
TIGER (wood)	Feb 5, 1962 – Jan 24, 1963
RABBIT (wood)	Jan 25, 1963 – Feb 12, 1964
DRAGON (earth)	Feb 13, 1964 – Feb 1, 1965
SNAKE (fire)	Feb 2, 1965 – Jan 20, 1966
HORSE (fire)	Jan 21, 1966 – Feb 8, 1967
SHEEP (earth)	Feb 9, 1967 – Jan 29, 1968
MONKEY (metal)	Jan 30, 1968 – Feb 16, 1969
ROOSTER (metal)	Feb 17, 1969 – Feb 5, 1970
DOG (earth)	Feb 6, 1970 – Jan 26, 1971
BOAR (water)	Jan 27, 1971 – Feb 14, 1972
RAT (water)	Feb 15, 1972 – Feb 2, 1973
OX (earth)	Feb 3, 1973 – Jan 22, 1974
TIGER (wood)	Jan 23, 1974 – Feb 10, 1975
RABBIT (wood)	Feb 11, 1975 – Jan 30, 1976
DRAGON (earth)	Jan 31, 1976 – Feb 17, 1977
SNAKE (fire)	Feb 18, 1977 – Feb 6, 1978
HORSE (fire)	Feb 7, 1978 – Jan 27, 1979
SHEEP (earth)	Jan 28, 1979 – Feb 15, 1980
MONKEY (metal)	Feb 16, 1980 – Feb 4, 1981
ROOSTER (metal)	Feb 5, 1981 – Jan 24, 1982
DOG (earth)	Jan 25, 1982 – Feb 12, 1983
BOAR (water)	Feb 13, 1983 – Feb 1, 1984

ANIMAL	WESTERN CALENDAR DATES
* Start of 60 year cycle	
RAT (water)	Feb 2, 1984 – Feb 19, 1985
OX (earth)	Feb 20, 1985 – Feb 8, 1986
TIGER (wood)	Feb 9, 1986 – Jan 28, 1987
RABBIT (wood)	Jan 29, 1987 – Feb 16, 1988
DRAGON (earth)	Feb 17, 1988 – Feb 5, 1989
SNAKE (fire)	Feb 6, 1989 – Jan 26, 1990
HORSE (fire)	Jan 27, 1990 – Feb 14, 1991
SHEEP (earth)	Feb 15, 1991 – Feb 3, 1992
MONKEY (metal)	Feb 4, 1992 – Jan 22, 1993
ROOSTER (metal)	Jan 23, 1993 – Feb 9, 1994
DOG (earth)	Feb 10, 1994 – Jan 30, 1995
BOAR (water)	Jan 31, 1995 – Feb 18, 1996
RAT (water)	Feb 19, 1996 – Feb 6, 1997
OX (earth)	Feb 7, 1997 – Jan 27, 1998
TIGER (wood)	Jan 28, 1998 – Feb 15, 1999
RABBIT (wood)	Feb 16, 1999 – Feb 4, 2000
DRAGON (earth)	Feb 5, 2000 – Jan 23, 2001
SNAKE (fire)	Jan 24, 2001 – Feb 11, 2002
HORSE (fire)	Feb 12, 2002 – Jan 31, 2003
SHEEP (earth)	Feb 1, 2003 – Jan 21, 2004
MONKEY (metal)	Jan 22, 2004 – Feb 8, 2005
ROOSTER (metal)	Feb 9, 2005 – Jan 28, 2006
DOG (earth)	Jan 29, 2006 – Feb 17, 2007
BOAR (water)	Feb 18, 2007 – Feb 6, 2008

index